T0024154

TOP**10**
CORFU AND THE
IONIAN ISLANDS

Top 10 Corfu and the Ionian Islands Highlights

The Top 10 of Everything

CONTENTS

Corfu and the Ionian Islands Area by Area

Streetsmart

Within each Top 10 list in this book, no hierarchy of quality or popularity is implied. All 10 are, in the editor's opinion, of roughly equal merit.

Title page, front cover and spine
Aerial view of the church of Panagia Vlacherna and Mouse Island in Kanóni, Corfu town
Back cover, clockwise from top left
The Achilleion Palace, picturesque Paleokastrítsa Bay on Corfu island, the lake of Melissáni Cave, a typical narrow street in Corfu

The rapid rate at which the world is changing is constantly keeping the DK Eyewitness team on our toes. While we've worked hard to ensure that this edition of Corfu and the Ionian Islands is accurate and up-to-date, we know that opening hours alter, standards shift, prices fluctuate, places close and new ones pop up in their stead. So, if you notice we've got something wrong or left something out, we want to hear about it. Please get in touch at **travelguides@dk.com**

Welcome to
Corfu and the Ionian Islands

With beautiful beaches, magnificent natural wonders and plentiful sunshine, the Ionian Islands offer a Mediterranean getaway like no other, whether you're seeking a beach holiday, a short break or a hiking trip. With DK Eyewitness Top 10 Corfu and the Ionian Islands, they're yours to explore.

Elegant **Corfu Old Town**, the spectacular **Achílleion Palace** and the wildlife haven of **Korissíon Lagoon** are just some of the must-see sights of Corfu. The neighbouring islands of **Paxí** and **Antipaxí**, with sandy beaches, picturesque towns and turquoise waters, are sublime.

Highlights of **Lefkáda** include scenic villages like **Nikiana** and **Lefkáda Town**, with its labyrinth of narrow streets lined with colourful homes. For the adventurous, there are waterfalls at **Nydrí** and windsurfing courses at **Vasilikí**. Neighbouring **Kefaloniá** is famous for its atmospheric capital, **Argostóli**, and its natural wonders: **Drogaráti Cave**, **Mýrtou Bay** and **Melissáni Lake** are sights not to be missed. Pretty **Ithaki**, believed to be where King Odysseus lived, lies off its shores.

Completing the archipelago is **Zákynthos**, an island with a coastline so spectacular that it has appeared on the cover of countless brochures. Who could forget the iconic **Navagio Beach** with its shipwreck, or the fabulous **Blue Caves**?

Whether you are visiting for a weekend or a week, our Top 10 guide brings together the best of everything Corfu and the Ionian Islands have to offer, from lush Paxí to historic Zákynthos. The guide has useful tips throughout, from seeking out what's free to places off the beaten track plus six easy-to-follow itineraries designed to tie together a clutch of sights in a short space of time. Add inspiring photography and detailed maps, and you've got the essential pocket-sized travel companion. **Enjoy the book, and enjoy Corfu and the Ionian Islands.**

Clockwise from top: **Palaio Frourio overlooking Corfu Old Town, statue at the Achílleion Palace in Corfu, Monastery of St Gerasímos at Kefaloniá, Pórto Katsiki Beach in Lefkáda, icon at the Monastery of Faneroménis in Lefkáda, Kefaloniá's Fiskárdo harbour, Vathý Bay in Ithaki**

Exploring Corfu and the Ionian Islands

With some stunning natural wonders, as well as several spectacular palaces and castles and many unspoiled villages, the Ionians are rich in beauty, culture and history. A two-day visit to Corfu gives a taste of the archipelagos, while the island of Paxí provides a starting point to explore the other islands on a longer stay.

Corfu's Achílleion Palace is one of the most popular attractions on the island.

Two Days on Corfu

Day ❶
MORNING
Admire Asiatic Art in the **Palace of St Michael and St George** in **Corfu Old Town**, and then vist the **Palaio Frourio** (see pp14–15). Stroll around **Plateia Spianáda** and take a break in a café at the **Liston** for lunch (see pp12–13).
AFTERNOON
See the **Dimarchio**, St Spyrídon's tall belfry and the **Antivouniotissa Museum's** Byzantine riches. Explore the **Neo Frourio** (see pp12–13). Dine at the elegant **Venetian Well** (see p73).

Day ❷
MORNING
Take the coast road to **Mon Repos** (see pp16–17) and on to the stunning **Achílleion Palace** (see pp18–19). Then, drive inland to the tranquil **Korissíon Lagoon** (see pp20–21). Make for **Pélekas** (see p67) and grab lunch at **Agnes Restaurant** (see p54). Look out for **Gardiki Castle** (see p66) en route.

AFTERNOON
Visit Paleokastrítsa and see the Angelókastro on the headland before stopping at Sidári to take the Wildlife Walk. End the day with a swim at the idyllic Battaria beach in Kassiópi, followed by an evening of 1960s music at Angelos Bar (see p72).

Seven Days in the Ionian Islands

Day ❶
From **Corfu Town**, take a day cruise to **Gäios, Paxí** (see p65). Marvel at the magnificent caves in Paxí, accessible by boat, then spend the afternoon swimming in the pristine turquoise waters of **Antipaxí** (see p63). Tours around the two islands are a great way to see further sights.

Day ❷
Catch an early ferry to Igoumenitsa and drive down the west coast of the mainland, passing by Syvota, Párga and Preveza. A causeway links

Antipaxí is a picturesque haven of beautiful beaches and turquoise seas.

The Blue Caves are an awesome natural wonder that can be seen by boat in northern Zákynthos.

road to iconic **Mýrtou Bay** *(see pp28–9)*. Stop by the Cyclopean walls of ancient Krani en route to **Argostóli** *(see pp26–7)*, then dine at **Patsouras** *(see p93)*.

Day ➎
Cross the island to explore two wonders of nature, the **Drogaráti Cave** and the **Melissáni Lake** and cave *(see pp30–31)* in **Sámi**. Take a boat trip to **Piso Aetós** *(see p87)* on Ithaki, believed to be the site of Odysseus's palace. Enjoy fine dining at **Sirens Restaurant** in Vathý *(see p95)*.

Day ➏
Return to **Sámi** *(see p85)* and head for **Pessada** *(see p88)*. Look out for Póros and the Monastery of Sissia en route. Take a ferry to **Agios Nikólaos** in Zákynthos. You'll catch sight of Cape Skinári, home of the magnificent **Blue Caves** *(see p97)*, as you approach.

Day ➐
Explore **Zákynthos Town** *(see pp32–3)*, a place of arcaded streets and fishing boats. Don't miss its famous **Church of Agios Dionýsios** *(see p33)* and the pre-earthquake model of the town in the **Byzantine Museum** *(see pp34–5)*.

Lefkáda with the mainland. See the ruins of **Sánta Mávra** overlooking the channel in **Lefkáda Town**.

Day ➌
Start your day in **Nikiana** *(see p75)* to see fishers bringing their catches ashore and continue on to **Nydrí** *(see p76)* for its splendid waterfalls. Take a boat trip to **Meganísi** *(see p77)* and back. Make haste to **Porto Katsiki Beach** *(see p76)* for a sunset swim.

Day ➍
Board the early ferry from Vasilikí to **Fiskárdo** *(see p86)* in Kefaloniá, known for its lovely pastel-coloured Venetian buildings. From here, take the coast

Top 10 Corfu and the Ionian Islands Highlights

Sunset over the Venetian-style harbourfront in Corfu Old Town

TOP 10 Corfu and the Ionian Islands Highlights

The widely scattered Ionian Islands, which lie off the western coast of mainland Greece, include Corfu (Kerkyra in Greek), Paxí, Antipaxí, Lefkáda, Kefaloniá, Ithaki and Zákynthos. The most verdant of all the Greek islands, they have great beaches and stunning caves, and offer a fabulous array of attractions.

Sidári
Kassiópi
See Around Corfu Town map, right
Gouvia
Glyfáda
Corfu
Mesongí
5
Korisíon Lagoon

Corfu Old Town ①

A UNESCO World Heritage Site, the oldest part of Corfu Town is a blend of architectural styles. It has imposing fortresses, a French-style arcaded terrace, the tranquil Plateia Spianáda and the elegant Palace of St Michael and St George.

② Palaio Frourio, Corfu Town

The Old Fortress, largely built by the Venetians in the 14th century, is Corfu Town's most distinctive landmark. The Byzantine Collection within its main gate contains impressive icons and frescos (see pp14–15).

③ Mon Repos Estate, Corfu

Sir Frederick Adam, a British Lord High Commissioner of the Ionians, built Mon Repos, which later became the summer home of the Greek royals. Major archaeological finds lie within its grounds (see pp16–17).

④ Achílleion Palace, Corfu

Built for Empress Elisabeth of Austria in the 1890s, this palace later became the home of Germany's Kaiser Wilhelm II. Marvel at the paintings and personal belongings of the palace's former owners (see pp18–19).

⑤ Korissíon Lagoon, Corfu

This freshwater lagoon, to the south of Corfu, is separated from the sea by sand dunes. A wildlife haven, it's a nature lover's paradise (see pp20–21).

Around Corfu Town

Corfu **1** **2** Palaio
Old Town   Frourio

3 Mon Repos
Estate

Chrisida   • Kanóni

• Kalafatiónes   • Pontikonísi

0 km   3   Achílleion
0 miles   3   **4** Palace

6 Lefkáda Town

Known for its unusual timber-framed buildings clad with colourful metal sheets, the town also has charming narrow streets, classic tavernas, quirky museums and a busy harbour (see pp24–5).

7 Argostóli, Kefaloniá

Pretty Argostóli boasts Neo-Classical mansions and fine squares with art galleries and cafés. Rebuilt after the 1953 earthquake, it is now Kefaloniá's trendy capital (see pp26–7).

8 Mýrtou Bay Area, Kefaloniá

Described as one of the most beautiful beaches in the world, Mýrtou Bay is famed for its turquoise sea, dazzling white sand and lush surroundings. Nearby are the pretty villages of Divarata and Agia Effimia (see pp28–9).

9 Caves of Kefaloniá

The impressive caves of Kefaloniá include Drogaráti cave, with its amazing rock formations, and the subterranean Melissáni cave and lake (see pp30–31).

10 Zákynthos Town

The capital of Zákynthos, this elegant town is full of Venetian-style architecture, with Neo-Classical buildings and large squares. After the devastating earthquake of 1953, Zákynthos Town was rebuilt in its original style (see pp32–3).

Map labels:

goumenitsa

• Párga

Paxí
• Gáios

Antipaxí

GREECE

Ionian Sea

Lefkáda Town **6**

Lefkáda   • Nikiana
              • Nydrí

Vasiliki •

Fiskárdo •   • Frikes
Kefaloniá *Ithaki*
Mýrtou Bay Area **8** • Vathý

Caves of Kefaloniá **9** • Sámi

Argostóli **7**   • Póros
           • Pessáda

Agios Nikólaos •
Zákynthos   • Katastári
         Zákynthos Town **10**

0 kilometres 25
0 miles   25

• Keri

TOP 10 ⭐ Corfu Old Town

With its cobbled plazas and tiny alleyways dating back to Roman times, Corfu Old Town exudes old-world charm. Palaces, museums, fortresses, gourmet restaurants, traditional tavernas, cultural venues and a lively harbour combine to give the town its inimitable character. It also has an eclectic architectural heritage, including Venetian fortresses, elegant British mansions and beautiful arcades reminisent of the finest in Paris.

3 Antivouniotissa Museum

Housed in the Church of Panagia (Our Lady) Antivouniotissa, this museum has a superb collection of Byzantine and post-Byzantine icons and treasures.

1 Palace of St Michael and St George

This building (above) was once home to the Greek royal family. At the forefront of local history for decades, it now houses the Museum of Asiatic Art.

2 Casa Parlante

Set in a Neo-Classical building, Corfu's patrician Venetian past is brought to life in this lively museum (left) as animated figures recreate the everyday life of a well-to-do Corfiot family in the 19th century.

4 Plateia Spianáda

A haven for anyone who likes to read, run or just take refuge from the heat, this is the town's largest square. It is divided in two by Viktoros Dousmani Street to create Ano Plateia and Kato Plateia.

5 Neo Frourio

The Venetians built this mighty fort in the 16th century to strengthen the town's defences. The Greek navy occupied it for many years and it is now open to the public.

NEED TO KNOW

Palace of St Michael and St George: MAP Q5; Plateia Spianáda. Museum of Asiatic Art: 26610 30443; open summer: 8am–8pm daily; winter 8:30am–3pm Wed–Mon; adm summer €6, winter €3

Casa Parlante: MAP P5; Nikiforou Theotoki 16; 26610 49190; open Mar–Nov: 10am–6pm Mon–Sat; adm €8

Antivouniotissa Museum: MAP P4; Prosforou 30; 26610 38313; open

summer: 8am–7:30pm daily; winter: 8:30am–3pm Tue–Sun; adm €4, concessions €2

Neo Frourio: MAP P1; Plateia Solomóu; open summer: 8:30am–3pm daily

Church of St Spyrídon: Map P5; Ag Spyridonos; 26610 33059, open 10am–1pm daily

■ Liston, Corfu's historic arcade is an ideal destination for refreshments.

6 Liston

An iconic Old Town sight, the Liston (above) was built in 1807 by Frenchman Mathieu de Lesseps. Known for its arcaded terraces and stylish cafés, it is a fine example of Napoleonic-period architecture. The terrace was inspired by the Rue de Rivoli in Paris.

THE MÁNOS COLLECTION

The focus of Corfu Old Town's Museum of Asiatic Art, the Mános Collection comprises 11,000 pieces of Chinese, Japanese and Korean furnishings, ceramics and weapons, plus some miniature works of art. Corfiot diplomat Grigórios Mános (1850–1928) amassed the fascinating collection during his travels and helped establish the museum.

7 Maitland Monument

Set in Plateia Spianáda, this 19th-century monument (below) is redolent of a Roman rotunda. It was built to commemorate the life of Sir Thomas Maitland, the first Lord High Commissioner of the Ionians (1815–23) during the British administration.

8 Old Port

Once an integral part of Corfu Town's fortifications, the ancient Old Port is one of the prettiest places in the area. Small cruise boats and ferries anchor here, while the larger ones go to the more modern New Port, a little to the east.

9 Church of St Spyrídon

Named after Corfu's patron saint, St Spyrídon, whose remains lie here in a silver coffin, this 16th-century church is an Old Town landmark. It has a distinct red-topped campanile with bells that ring out at regular intervals.

10 Dimarchio

The Dimarchio, or Town Hall, is a Venetian-style building that was once the San Giacomo theatre, a favourite haunt of the island's nobility.

Corfu Old Town

Corfu Old Town as seen from the New Fortress

TOP 10 ⭐ Palaio Frourio, Corfu Town

Once home to almost 2,000 people, the Palaio Frourio (Old Fortress) stands on a peninsula jutting eastward into the Ionian sea. Founded by the Byzantines in the 11th century, the fortress was strengthened in the 14th century by the Venetians. Its defences withstood Ottoman sieges in 1537, 1571 and 1716. Barracks, a military hospital and other buildings were added during the 19th-century British occupation. Known to the ancient Greeks as Koryfo, the site lent its name to Corfu Town and eventually the whole island.

2 Church of Agios Georgios

With its Doric columns and portico, the elegant Church of St George **(left)**, built by the British in 1840, resembles a Classical temple. It became an Orthodox church after the British left Corfu.

1 Schulenburg Statue

A marble statue of the fortress's most famous defender, Count Schulenburg, by the Venetian sculptor Antonio Corradini, stands close to the footbridge that leads to the Palaio Frourio.

3 Main Gate and Contrafossa

The Venetians dug the contrafossa, a defensive moat, to separate the promontory on which the fortress stands from the rest of Corfu. A footbridge spans the contrafossa leading to the main gate. It is flanked on either side by two large bastions.

4 Chapel of Madonna dei Carmini

Built by the Catholic Carmelite order between 1636 and 1671, this simple chapel has a roof supported by columns that probably came from an earlier Greek temple. It is open for temporary exhibitions of historic works of art, maps and documents.

NEED TO KNOW

MAP Q1 ■ Access from Viktoro Dousmani ■ 26610 27935

Open Apr–Oct: 8am–7.30pm daily; Nov–Mar: 8am–4pm daily; adm €6

■ The Old Fortress café-bar serves cold drinks, coffee and snacks, such as giros platters and salads, and has free Wi-Fi.

■ On the Mandraki quayside, the elegant Corfu Sailing Club Restaurant *(26610 38763; open Apr–Oct: 12:30pm–11:30pm)* serves Greek-Mediterranean cuisine and has an extensive local wine list.

■ There is a small pebbly beach just west of Mandraki Harbour where it is possible to swim and cool off after exploring the fortress.

8 Clock Tower
The elegant Venetian bell tower **(left)** with its four clock faces and pink-painted walls stands below the Castella Terra. Its bells were tolled to warn of approaching enemies such as Turkish pirates or an Ottoman fleet, as well as to ring out the hour.

5 Byzantine Collection
Built into the main gate, the Byzantine Collection contains a small but impressive collection of religious works of art including mosaics, sculptures and frescoes.

6 Public Library
The imposing historic British barracks, built to house soldiers of a garrison that numbered up to 1,600 men, now houses a public library which has a valuable collection of Venetian manuscripts, rare books and historic maps and prints.

7 Castella Terra
It takes 20–30 minutes to climb the stone steps to the top of the inner fort that the Venetians called Castella Terra. A polygonal stone well can be seen close to the top. This is the highest point of the Palaio Frourio, with breathtaking views.

9 Akra Sidero Lighthouse
Built by the British in 1828 in the centre of the citadel, this round stone lighthouse with its green roof still guides ships in and out of Corfu's harbour, though it is a little dilapidated.

10 Mandraki Harbour
The fortified city's original harbour, on the north side of the islet **(below)**, is now the base of the Corfu Sailing Club and is filled with elegant sailing yachts.

JOHANN MATTHIAS VON DER SCHULENBURG

A Prussian aristocrat and soldier, Schulenburg (1661–1747) was recruited by the Venetians to defend the Palaio Frourio in the 1714–18 Ottoman–Venetian War. The fortress survived a 7-week siege in 1716, when a Turkish fleet was finally driven away by a storm. When the war ended, Venice retained the Ionian Islands, but lost its possessions on the mainland.

Palaio Frourio floorplan

🔟 ⭐ Mon Repos Estate, Corfu

With its extensive lush gardens set on the hill of Analipsis at Kanóni, the Mon Repos Estate is a tranquil haven. Created during British rule by the second Lord High Commissioner of the Ionians, Sir Frederick Adam, the estate later became the summer home of the Greek royal family, and the birthplace of Prince Philip, the Duke of Edinburgh. It is also famous for being the site of Palaeopolis, the island's ancient city, and visitors can see the ruins of ancient buildings in the grounds.

1 Mon Repos Villa

The elegant Neo-Classical villa **(above)** with rounded porticoes was built in 1824. It was designed by Sir George Whitmore, the architect of the Palace of St Michael and St George. Mon Repos is now a museum.

2 The Estate Gardens

Laid over 100 ha (250 acres), the gardens **(below)** bring together lavish Mediterranean shrubs, flowers, lawns, trees and impressive historical remains – look out for the ruins of three Doric temples.

3 Ruins of the Temple of Hera

The remains of this Doric temple lie close to the villa. Dating to the 7th century BC, it is said to have been ancient Corfu's largest temple. The ruins suggest it was built using advanced architectural methods of the day.

4 Roman Baths

The Roman baths on the estate include an underfloor hypocaust for the circulation of hot air. The baths date back to around AD 200 and the reign of Emperor Septimus Severus.

SIR FREDERICK ADAM

Sir Frederick Adam (1781–1853) became the second Lord High Commissioner of the Ionians in 1824 after a distinguished career in the British army. Mon Repos was built as a gift for his wife Nina, born Diamatina Palatino, who was from Cyprus. The couple lived in the villa only for a few years before Sir Frederick was appointed the governor of Madras, India, in 1832.

6 Ruins of St Kerkyra Basilica

Dedicated to St Kerkyra, this basilica **(above)** was an important church in the 5th century AD. Built to resemble a crucifix from above, its entrance porticos and the transept are still worth seeing.

7 Alkinoos Harbour

The remains of a harbour, named after a king from Homer's *The Odyssey*, were found at the same time as an ancient dock-yard. Nearby are remains of what may have been the homes of merchants.

8 Museum of Palaeopolis

Housed within the villa, this superb museum has ancient archaeological treasures, such as Doric columns, alongside refined clothing, household items and furniture from the time of British rule.

5 Hellenistic Agora

The agora was at the heart of the island's commercial activity in ancient times. Here, traders used to stand on large stone slabs offering their wares.

9 Ruins of the Temple of Apollo

The ruins of what is considered to have been a fabulous temple can be found in the villa grounds **(above)**. Built in a Doric style, it is believed to have been dedicated to the god Apollo, who was the son of Zeus.

10 Doric Temple of Kardaki

Dating from the late 6th century BC, this is the island's best surviving ancient temple. It was discovered in 1822 on the estate's south-eastern slope in what is today known as Kardaki.

NEED TO KNOW

MAP Q3 ■ Kanóni, Corfu Town

Mon Repos Estate: 26610 41369; open 8am–sunset daily

Mon Repos Villa: 26610 41369; open 8:30am–3:30pm Wed–Mon; adm €4, concessions €2

■ Ruins of St Kerkyra Basilica, Hellenistic Agora, Alkinoos Harbor and the Roman Baths lie just outside the estate.

■ An information board directs you to the sights.

■ Water is available but there are no refreshment stops, so carry snacks.

TOP 10 ★ Achílleion Palace, Corfu

This Neo-Classical palace was built in the late 1890s for the Empress Elisabeth of Austria, known as Princess Sissi. The work of respected Italian architect Raphael Carita, it was used as a retreat by the empress, who adored Corfu. Following her assassination by an anarchist in 1898, the palace remained empty until Germany's Kaiser Wilhelm II bought it in 1907. Today, it is one of Corfu's most popular sights.

The Main Hall ①
The entrance hall **(right)** to the palace is dominated by a massive marble staircase and fabulous ceiling decorations, the most notable being the *Four Seasons* fresco.

② Four Seasons
Painted by Galoppi, a 19th-century Italian artist, the fabulous *Four Seasons* fresco is an impressive sight. The painting depicts female figures who represent the seasons and is said to have been one of Sissi's favourite palace features.

③ Peristyle of the Muses
This colonnade has an understated elegance. Its pillars and statues surround an inner courtyard and lead down some steps to the beautiful gardens **(below)**.

④ Kaiser's Bridge
This arched bridge was requested by Kaiser Wilhelm II to make a beach across the road more accessible. Parts of it were destroyed during World War II when Corfu was under German occupation, but it remains an important architectural landmark.

5 Kaiser's Room

Known as Kaiser's Room, the office of Kaiser Wilhelm II, the very last emperor of Germany, is located on the ground floor. Displayed in the room are the Kaiser's personal belongings, including documents, furniture, portraits and a collection of medals.

6 Empress Elisabeth's Catholic Chapel

This tiny chapel (right), featuring an icon of the Virgin Mary, is where Princess Sissi is said to have prayed. It lies just off the main entrance hall of the palace, and is decorated with a beautiful ceiling fresco.

7 Palace Collection of Paintings

The palace has a rich collection of paintings by artists of the period that includes portraits of Sissi and Wilhelm II, and *Achilles' Triumph* (above) by Austrian artist Franz Matsch (1861–1942).

ACHÍLLES

The empress Elisabeth dedicated the Achílleion Palace to the ancient warrior Achílles, famous for his role in the Battle of Troy, where he killed the Trojan hero Hector. As the story goes, the newborn Achílles was immersed in the River Styx by his mother. This made him invincible, apart from the heel where she had held him. Achílles survived many battles before being fatally shot in the heel by Paris, brother of Hector.

8 Statues of Goddesses in the Gardens

Statues of important Greek mythological figures also adorn the palace's gardens. Among them are the goddesses Artemis, the deity of forests and hunting, who is seen standing upright and defiant, and the alluring Aphrodite, goddess of love and beauty.

9 Statues of Hera and Zeus

Princess Sissi adored Greek mythology and commissioned statues of gods to be placed around the palace. These include the statues of Hera and Zeus, which stand at the foot of the majestic marble staircase leading up to the first floor.

10 Statue of the Dying Achílles

One of the most impressive statues in the gardens is the *Dying Achílles* (right), by the 19th-century German sculptor Ernst Herter. The large bronze depicts the wounded Achílles trying to remove an arrow from his heel and forms the garden's centrepiece.

NEED TO KNOW

MAP D4 ■ Gastouri, on the outskirts of Corfu Town ■ 26610 56210 ■ www.achillion-corfu.gr

Open Apr–Oct: 8am–7pm daily; Nov–Mar: 9am–3:30pm daily

Adm €7

■ There are wonderful views of southern Corfu from the hilltop gardens above the palace.

■ There are a few tavernas in the village and a kiosk near the entrance to the palace that sells soft drinks and snacks.

TOP10 ⭐ Korissíon Lagoon, Corfu

The Korissíon Lagoon in southern Corfu is a sublimely tranquil spot. A protected area, it is separated from the Ionian Sea by sand dunes dotted with juniper bushes. The beaches of Agios Georgios, Issos and Halikounas are on its shores, while an ancient cedar forest provides a backdrop. The large brackish lagoon and its surroundings provide habitats for wildlife, trees and flowers, including orchids and a rare species of lily. It is an important stop for migrating birds from Africa to Europe; you may also see sandpipers, ducks, seagulls, swans and, if you're lucky, Scops owls or buzzards flying overhead.

① Halikounas Beach

Located on the narrow strip of shoreline separating Korissíon Lagoon from the sea, isolated Halikounas Beach **(above)** is long, wide and sandy. It is dotted with juniper bushes that give it a wild feel. There are no tavernas here, only enthusiasts enjoying the flora and fauna.

② Grava Cave

This large cave close to Halikounas Beach was only discovered a few years back. It contained ancient animal bones, along with some stone tools and primitive vessel-like items, crafted by communities that are believed to have lived here two million years ago in Palaeolithic times.

③ Agios Georgios Beach (St Georges)

This long, wide beach **(above)**, bordered by cypress trees and olive groves, lies to the south of the lagoon and is a popular spot for sunbathers. The adjacent town of Agios Georgios is a small resort with accommodation and tavernas.

④ Gardiki Castle

The remains of the Byzantine fort of Gardiki Castle **(below)** overlook the lagoon. It was one of three built in the 13th century to defend Corfu. The others are at Kassiópi and Angelókastro, near Palaiokastrítsa.

Issos Beach 5

This beautiful sandy beach **(right)** is close to the lagoon. It is quiet and famous for its stunning sunsets. The beach is a favourite with locals and has good watersports, especially windsurfing and kite surfing, which take advantage of its strong offshore winds.

7 Bioporos Ecological Farm

This super eco-farm, which is open to visitors and offers farm stays, has a great restaurant where local dishes are prepared using organic ingredients from the estate, such as vegetables, olives and honey. You can also watch bread being baked in the restaurant's wood oven.

8 Local Flora

There are said to be no fewer than twelve species of orchid and lily around the lagoon, the most notable being the rare lily *Pancratium maritimum*. This white flower grows on the sand dunes and has a pleasant scent, especially on still summer evenings.

9 Livadiotis Winery

The lagoon is surrounded by vineyards and it is from here that the flavoursome Protected Geographical Indication (PGI) Halicouna wine is produced. A dry white with fruity aromas, it is made from the kakotrygis grape grown almost exclusively in this part of Corfu.

10 Cedars and Junipers

The Korissíon Lagoon is famous for the forests of cedar trees and juniper bushes found around its beaches. The forests have developed over millennia and add a different habitat for the wildlife and birdlife that thrives in the natural ecosystem of the lagoon.

NEED TO KNOW

MAP D5

Bioporos Ecological Farm: Korissíon Lagoon, 49080, Corfu; open Mar–Nov (restaurant: Jun–Sep) www.bioporos.gr

Livadiotis Winery: Thesi Halikouna, Agios Matheos, Kastellana, Messi, 49084, Corfu; 23710 95455; www.ktima-livadioti.com

■ The Korissíon Lagoon, or the "great lake" is in southwest Corfu. It is best reached from the west coast town of Pélekas, or cross-country from the east coast town of Mesongí.

■ There are few facilities other than at the small resort of Agios Georgios, a handful of beach bars, the Bioporos Ecological Farm and the Livadiotis Winery, home of the Greek wine Halicouna.

6 Migratory Birds

While you will see seagulls, ducks and swans all year round at Korissíon Lagoon, in spring and autumn you might also catch sight of some migratory birds on their journey between Africa and central Europe. These include swallows, the majestic black Great Cormorant **(right)** and the white Great Egret.

Following pages Main Hall of the Achilleion Palace, Corfu

🔟 ⭐ Lefkáda Town

Lying on a promontory around a natural harbour in Lefkáda's north, the island's capital has a modern appearance as a result of recurrent earthquake damage and the resulting reconstruction of its buildings. The town has a sophisticated, relaxed feel, and offers everything from tiny streets and squares to great waterfront restaurants and elegant shopping along Dorpfeld, its pedestrianized street. Life here revolves around the harbour area and lively marina. The town is linked to the Greek mainland by two small bridges over a channel.

① The Marina
Located on the town's east side, Lefkáda marina **(right)** is one of the largest in the Ionians. It has attractive bars, restaurants and shops, and offers all the facilities required for berthing vessels.

② Pantazis Kontomixis Ethnological Museum
This small but exquisite museum **(above)** houses traditional clothes worn by the Lefkádites over the centuries. It also displays textiles, looms and old photographs.

④ Post-Byzantine Art Gallery
Housed in a classical building, this art gallery is part of Lefkáda Town's library. It has books, some manuscripts and a superb collection of post-Byzantine art and icons dating from the 17th to the 19th centuries.

⑤ Monastery of Faneroménis
Set on a hill overlooking Lefkáda's harbour, this monastery was founded in the 17th century. The present building is more recent. Its ecclesiastical museum has several icons, the oldest of which is from the 15th century.

③ Colourful Architecture
After the 1948 earthquake destroyed most of Lefkáda Town's old buildings, they were rebuilt with timber frames covered with colourful metal sheets.

Lefkáda Town

13 km (8 miles) ⑥
3 km (2 miles) ⑩
⑨
④
SIKELIANOU
②
SP. GAZI
1 km (0.6 miles) ⑧
DIMARCHOU GIANNOULIANOU
PANAGOULI PANAGOU
N. ZAMBELIOU
IOANNOU MELA
⑦
⑤
3 km (2 miles)
MERARHIAS
GOLEMI
①

6 Mýlos Beach

For a great day trip head to beautiful Mýlos beach (above), which is nestled in a scenic lagoon. It can be accessed by boat or over the headland west of Lefkáda Town.

7 Phonograph Museum

This museum has an unusual private collection of antique radios and gramophones. There are musical instruments and sheet music, as well as some personal items.

TRADITIONAL DRESS

The country has many variations of traditional attire. Lefkádite men used to wear a *bourzana*, comprising short pants and a white shirt. Women wore a full dress, called a *katolo*. No longer worn every day, these clothes can be seen at festivals. Lefkáda is also known for its rich silk wedding dresses and traditional groom's outfit of felt trousers, a white shirt and *geleki* or waistcoat.

8 Sánta Mávra Fortress Ruins

Dominating the skyline near the channel are the ruins of the early 14th-century castle of Sánta Mávra (below), which was built to defend the town.

9 Archaeological Museum

Although it looks modern, the town has a long history. Its Archaeological Museum displays artifacts from all over the island that date as far back as the early Bronze Age.

10 Agios Ioannis Beach

Lying just outside town, Agios Ioannis is one of the finest beaches on the island. With golden sand, a vivid turquoise sea and a frequent breeze, it has become known as a windsurfing paradise.

NEED TO KNOW

MAP J1

Pantazis Kontomixis Ethnological Museum: T Stratou; 26450 25497; call for timings; adm €2

Post-Byzantine Art Gallery: Rontogianni; 26450 22502; open 8:30am–1:30pm Tue–Sat (also 5–7pm Tue); adm €2

Monastery of Faneromenís: Frini; 26450 21305; open 8am–2pm and 4–7pm daily

Mýlos Beach: **MAP H1**

Phonograph Museum: Kalkani 14; 69974 93010; open 10am–2pm & 7–10pm daily; adm (donation)

Sánta Mávra Fortress Ruins: 26450 26576; open summer: 8am–8pm Wed–Mon, winter: 8am–3pm Wed–Mon; adm €3

Archaeological Museum: Ag Sikelianou; 26450 21635; open summer: 8am–3pm Wed–Mon; winter: 8:30am–3pm Wed–Mon; adm €3, concessions €2

■ Ioannou Mela and Goulielmou Dorpfeld form the city's pedestrianized main thoroughfare. A choice of cafés and bars can be found here, and on Lefkáda's main square, Plateia Agiou Spyrodonos.

TOP 10 ⭐ Argostóli, Kefaloniá

Argostóli is a classic Greek town that hugs the shores of the Koutavos Lagoon, a protected nature reserve on Kefaloniá's southwest coast. It has been the island's capital since 1757, but the historic appearance of its buildings is deceptive. Neo-Classical mansions, fine churches, imposing government buildings and large open squares were created after the town was completely destroyed in the catastrophic earthquake of 1953. Today, life revolves around the bustling Plateia Vallianos, home to cafés and galleries, and the main shopping and commercial streets of Lithostróto and the tree-lined Rizospaston.

The beautiful waterfront of Argostóli

1 Argostóli Town Centre

Plateia Vallianos, a large, paved square full of palm trees and dominated by a statue of town benefactor Panagis Vallianos, lies at the heart of Argostóli. From here it's a short stroll to many key sites.

2 Koutavos Lagoon

Once a swamp, the Koutavos Lagoon (below) was dredged when the Drapanos Bridge was built. Now a protected nature reserve, it is a feeding ground for the loggerhead turtle. A pathway around it is popular with walkers and cyclists.

3 Napier Garden

Named after the British governor of Kefaloniá, General Sir Charles James Napier (1782–1853), who was instrumental in creating the garden in the 19th century, this tranquil spot on Koutoupi hill is famous for its extensive collection of trees and shrubs.

4 Katovothres

Located near the famed landmarks of Agioi Theodoroi church and lighthouse, Katovothres is a geological marvel. Here, sea water enters caverns, disappears underground and resurfaces 14 days later at Melissáni Lake and Karavomylos in the Sámi area.

5 Korgialeneios Library

Housed in a classical building designed to look as it did before the earthquake, the library holds around 55,000 books, manuscripts and icons saved in 1953. The oldest are Byzantine. Founded in 1924, the library is named after benefactor Marinos Korgialenios.

7 Drapanos Bridge

Constructed in 1813, this 690 m (2,264 ft) stone bridge **(left)** links Argostóli with the villages opposite the town. British governor Charles De Bosset began its construction, while successor Charles Napier completed it. The bridge is also known as De Bosset Bridge.

8 Lássi

A modern sprawl of mid-range hotels, restaurants and bars, Lássi is located on the outskirts of the capital. It has trendy tavernas, water-sports, sandy beaches and lovely views across the water to Lixóuri. Locals come here to unwind.

6 Korgialeneio Historical and Folklore Museum

The island's Venetian conquest in 1500 AD, along with the destruction and rebuilding of Argostóli after the 1953 earthquake is shown in exhibits displayed in this museum. Other exhibits include tools and costumes.

9 Agios Spyrídon

This church in Lithostróto **(right)** houses the gold iconostasis of the Cathedral of Argostóli, which was saved when the building fell in 1953. A memorial procession for the victims of the earthquake leaves from here every year.

ARGOSTÓLI AND THE 1953 EARTHQUAKE

On 12 August 1953, an earthquake measuring 7.2 on the Richter scale struck the southern Ionian Islands. It caused massive damage to the islands of Zákynthos and Kefaloniá, which is said to have risen 60 cm (24 in) above the seabed. Argostóli was flattened and its infrastructure damaged beyond repair. Hundreds died and the survivors lost their homes and livelihoods. The town has since been rebuilt to its original, traditional look. The inspiring story of how Argostóli rose from the rubble is told in the Korgialeneio Historical and Folklore Museum.

10 Agios Georgios (Kástro)

The capital of Kefaloniá until 1757, the ruins of 16th-century Venetian fortress of Agios Georgios, together with its pretty whitewashed village of Kástro, can be reached by a winding mountain road.

Argostóli, Kefaloniá

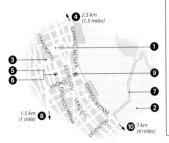

NEED TO KNOW

MAP G5

KTEL Kefalonias Bus Service: www.ktelkefalonias.gr/en

Korgialeneios Library: Ilia Zervou 12

Korgialeneio Historical and Folklore Museum: Ilia Zervou 12; 26710 28835; open 8:30am–3pm; adm €3

Agios Spyrídon: Lithostróto

■ A great spot for excellent traditional dishes is Palia Plaka (see p93)

Mýrtou Bay Area, Kefaloniá

With its iconic white crescent-shaped beach, bright turquoise sea and mountainous backdrop, Mýrtou Bay (Kolpos Mýrtou) has been voted one of the most beautiful bays in the world, and is certainly the most photographed in the Ionians. Often known as Myrtos, it is flanked by two mountains, Agia Dynati and Kalon Oros, and can be reached by a road of hairpin bends that descends sharply from the mountain village of Divarata. South of the bay lies the small yet bustling fishing village Agia Effimia.

Panoramic Views 1

One of the most stunning views of beautiful Mýrtou Bay **(right)** is from above, along the well-signposted road from the village of Sinióri. There is a special viewing area for visitors that offers sweeping views of the white beach, the surrounding verdant countryside and the brilliant blue sea.

2 Silver Birch Forests

The rural landscape on the hills above Mýrtou Bay is largely made up of forests of silver birch. This medium-sized deciduous tree can be recognized by its white trunk and pale green leaves, and is found only at higher altitudes on the island.

3 Divarata

The road down to Mýrtou Bay descends from Divarata, one of the small villages on Mount Agia Dynati. This scenic village has several tavernas and lies along the coast road from Kardakata to Fiskárdo.

4 Turquoise Sea

The sea's vivid blue colour is a result of the white-pebble seabed reflecting the light. The colour is intensified by the deeply shelving beach and the motion of the sea picking up tiny pebbles as it hits the shore.

5 Agia Effimia

Mýrtou Bay lies close to the traditional fishing village of Agia Effimia **(left)**, the capital of the Pylaros region. Agia Effimia is known for its lively nautical activity. From here, tour boats cruise along the coast, affording some of the best views of the bay.

 ### White Pebble Beach
The dazzling white beach **(above)** has been formed over millennia by the erosion of the cliffs enclosing the bay. The rock debris was deposited on the beach and worn down by the sea to form pebbles.

CAPTAIN CORELLI'S MANDOLIN
Mýrtou Bay famously featured in the 2001 film *Captain Corelli's Mandolin*, which was adapted from British novelist Louis de Bernières' 1994 novel of the same name. It tells of the eviction of the Italians by the Germans in World War II *(see p39)*. Although both film and book boosted tourism in the bay, it retains its idyllic nature and is protected from over-development.

Mýrtou Bay Area, Kefaloniá

NEED TO KNOW
MAP H4 ■ Near Divarata and Sinióri, Kefaloniá

■ The bay is protected from development. It has few facilities, other than basic refreshments.

■ The car park closest to the beach fills up quickly in summer so arrive early to secure a space.

Sheer Cliffs
The soaring cliffs of Mýrtou Bay are a photogenic highlight of the area. Made up of calcite-rich limestone, the white cliffs contrast sharply with the deep blue colour of the sea.

Mount Kalon Oros
Along with Agia Dynati, Kalon Oros forms a dramatic backdrop to the bay. At around 900 m (3,000 ft), it offers superb views. Look out for nearby pretty villages where local crafts and traditions still thrive.

Mount Agia Dynati
According to Greek lore, Agia Dynati was the rock that Titan leader, Cronus, dropped to earth. After Lefkáda's Mount Elati and Kefaloniá's Mount Aino, Agia Dynati, at 1,100 m (4,000 ft), is the third-highest mountain in the Ionian Islands.

Diving and Snorkelling Coves
With its tiny coves, caves and rocks **(below)**, Mýrtou Bay is a paradise for snorkellers and divers. Take care, however, as currents are strong and the seabed drops sharply.

TOP 10 ⭐ Caves of Kefaloniá

The spectacular caves of Kefaloniá are geological wonders with a beautiful interplay of light, water and stone. Three of the most interesting caves are open to visitors. A boat tour of the Melissáni cave is simply magical. The Zervati cave features brilliant blue lakes and the Drogkaráti cave, with its splendid mineral formations, has a chamber of such tremendous proportions and fine acoustics that it can be used to host concerts.

Melissáni Cave ①

Discovered by speleologist Gianni Petrochilo, in 1951, this cave **(right)** near Sámi is believed to have been the sanctuary of the god Pan. It is famous for its blue lake lit by the sun through a hole in its roof. The lake is fed from the sea via underground caves.

② Aghia Eleousa Cave

Remarkable only for the fact that it was created by nature, this cave is neither deep nor large. However, it does empty into a salt-water lake thought to be connected to the underground stream network that feeds Lake Melissáni.

③ Agios Gerasimos

Named after the patron saint of Kefaloniá, this cave **(below)** at Lássi is said to be where St Gerasimos lived when he first came to the island in 1560. A tiny chapel can still be seen in the cave.

④ Angalaki Cave

This enormous cave can be found along the main road leading north out of Sámi. Among its fascinating features are huge caverns, underground lakes and shelves along the walls formed by erosion of the rocks.

⑤ Zervati Cave

This cave has passages that descend deep into the earth. With Angalaki cave, it is one of the deepest in the area and has great caverns and underground lakes, many with submerged stalactites and stalagmites.

⑥ Aghia Theodori Cave

One of the lesser-known caves, Aghia Theodori is a deep shaft that leads to a small underground lake, thought to be home to a variety of fish and subterranean foliage.

7 Drogaráti Cave

Located near Sámi, this cave (left) is believed to be more than one million years old. Its natural wonders include the creatively named Royal Balcony – a natural platform where visitors can stand to admire stalactites and stalagmites. Here, too, is the famous Chamber of Exaltation, which has perfect acoustics and is used for musical concerts.

8 Sakkos Cave

Located in Skála, not far from the location of the ancient Temple of Apollo, this cave is comprised of two caverns linked by a tunnel, and has some magnificent stalactites and stalagmites. Fragments of pottery, implements and tools found here, as well as inscriptions, suggest it may have been a dwelling in ancient times.

9 Loizos Cave

This dramatic cave is believed to have been a place of worship for more than 2,000 years. The remains of a sanctuary that date to the 9th century BC were found here. Further excavations revealed artifacts that could be dated to the Mycenaen period, the Geometric period (900–700 BC) and the Roman period.

Caves of Kefaloniá

10 Faraklata Cave

This lesser-known cave lies on a mountain slope overlooking the Gulf of Argostóli, to the east of Faraklata village. It is a small, but challenging cave to explore. Excavations have revealed pottery that suggest it was a dwelling more than 2,000 years ago.

STALACTITES AND STALAGMITES

Stalactites thrive in a cave-like environment and hang from the ceiling of many caves in Kefaloniá. They are created by mineral deposits found in rain that seeps through rock and solidifies when it reaches air. They grow at a rate of around 10 mm (0.3 in) every 100 years. Stalagmites are the structures formed on the cave floor by drips from the stalactites above.

NEED TO KNOW

Melissáni Cave: **MAP H5**; near Sámi; open daily 8am–8pm; adm

Aghia Eleousa Cave: **MAP H5**; near Sámi

Agios Gerasimos Cave: **MAP G6**; Lássi

Angalaki Cave: **MAP H5**; near Sámi

Zervati Cave: **MAP H5**; near Sámi

Aghia Theodori Cave: **MAP H5**; near Sámi

Drogaráti Cave: **MAP H5**; near Sámi; open 8am–8pm daily; adm

Sakkos Cave: **MAP J6**; near Skála

Loizos Cave: **MAP G5**; near Kardakata

Faraklata Cave: Map H5; Faraklata

■ Try to visit early in the morning or late in the afternoon to avoid the crowds in the caves at the middle of the day.

■ The route down to the caves can be steep and the ground damp and slippery, so watch your step or ask for help.

TOP 10 ⭐ Around Zákynthos Town

The island's capital and principal port, reconstructed following a 1953 earthquake, retains its Venetian Neo-Classical character. With its beautiful squares, arcaded streets and lively harbor, Zákynthos Town is enchanting and the surrounding area is an unspoiled natural wonder. Zakynthos is a pioneer in eco-tourism, and the National Marine Park is just minutes from town.

① Ecclesiastical Museum
Housed in the Monastery of St Dionýsios, this museum **(above)** displays a valuable collection of icons from the Monastery of Strofades, home to St Dionýsios in the 16th century.

② Lomvardou Street
Known locally as Strata Marina, the esplanade that runs alongside the harbour has elegant buildings on one side and colourful boats on the other.

④ National Marine Park

Set up in 1999, the park is a protected habitat for local flora and fauna, including loggerhead sea turtles and Mediterranean monk seals. Visitors are asked to leave the nesting beaches after sunset, when the turtles emerge.

⑤ Byzantine Museum

One of the best collections of ecclesiastical art in Greece is on show at this museum (see pp34–5) in Plateia Solomóu. Its magnificent frescoes and icons are saved when the churches crumbled in the 1953 quake.

③ Venetian Fortress

Overlooking the town, this mid-17th-century fortress once played a key role defending the town. Look out for the Lions of St Markos inscription **(above)** over the entrance.

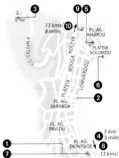

Zákynthos Town

Harbour of Zákynthos Town

8 Logothetis Organic Farm

This sustainable eco-tourism farm comprises traditional farmhouses, orchards and olive groves. Press your own olive oil, take a cooking class or explore the scenery here.

6 Church of Agios Nikolaos Molos

This pretty mid-16th century church is one of the few of Zákynthos's original Venetian buildings to have survived the 1953 earthquake.

7 Church of Agios Dionýsios

The impressive church of St Dionýsios **(below)** is dedicated to the island's patron saint, whose body lies here in a silver coffin. The church's Venetian bell tower is a town landmark.

9 Museum of Solomós

This museum celebrates the lives of prominent Zákynthiot citizens, most notably the 19th-century poet Dionysios Solomós **(above)**. It houses the poet's tomb and a collection of his manuscripts.

10 Helmi's Natural History Museum

Wonderful displays of butterflies, birds and sea shells offer an up-close experience of nature.

Byzantine Museum, Zákynthos Town

1 Model of Zákynthos Town
A fascinating exhibit, this 1:500 detailed scaled model by local 20th-century artist Yianni Manesi shows the layout and Venetian architecture of Zákynthos Town as it looked before the devastating earthquake of 1953.

Model of Zákynthos before 1953

2 Descent from the Cross
This fine painting of Christ being lowered from the cross after his crucifixion is from the church of St Andreas of the Gardens. Painted by Greek artist Nikólaos Kantounes, it's one of the museum's most prized exhibits.

3 St Demetrios of Kola Templon
Dated by its inscription to the year 1690, this beautifully carved and gilded templon (sanctuary screen) would have once stood between the congregation and the inner sanctuary and altar of the church of St Demetrios of Kola.

4 Sanctuary Door from Panagia Gavalousa
Depicting the Apostles Paul on the right panel holding a closed book, and Peter

on the left with an unopened scroll and keys in his hands, this well-preserved door was saved from the Panagia (Virgin) Gavalousa church. It has been dated to around 1570.

5 Birth of the Theotokos
The work of Nikólaos Doxaras, a much-admired 18th-century artist, this lavish painting once adorned the ceiling of the Phaneromeni church in Zákynthos Town. It shows St Anna on a couch with a newborn child and servants. They are watched over by winged angels encased in a cloud.

6 Hellenic and Byzantine Sculpture Collection
The museum has an extensive collection of sculptures, figurines and architectural remnants dating from the Hellenic and Byzantine periods. Each piece is subtly lit and displayed with an informative label.

7 Procession with the Relics of St Charalambos
Artist Ioánnis Korais painted this acclaimed work of art in 1756. It shows the social groups of the day – including children, women, men, priests and officials – in a procession with an icon of one of the island's

Sanctuary screen from the church of St Demetrios of Kola

saints, St Charalambos held aloft on a cathedra. The painting was rescued from the church of the same name.

 Panagia Amolyntos
The title translates to mean the "Immaculate Virgin", and this painting by Cretan Emmanuel Tzanes shows Mary holding the infant Christ. It once adorned the walls of the Phaneromeni Church in Zákynthos Town. Considered an important example of 17th-century art, it is one of the museum's main exhibits.

Panagia Amolyntos

⑨ Prophet David Portrait
The vibrant colours of Nikólaos Doxaras' 18th-century portrait of the Prophet David, are typical of the Heptanese school, which blended Venetian and orthodox influences.

⑩ Church of the Soter Wall Fresco
Dating from the 12th century, this is one of the oldest and most important exhibits here. It was rescued from the Church of the Soter (Saviour) in the town's Venetian fortress (the Kástro) and shows Saint Theodote with her children.

ZÁKYNTHOS'S HISTORY

Named after Zákynthos, the son of the Arcadian hero Dardanos of Troy, this island has a stormy past, according to myth. It was conquered by King Arkesios of Kefaloniá, then Odysseus of Ithaki before an alliance was formed with Athens during the First Peloponnesian War around 459 BC. Zákynthos came under Byzantine rule from around the 8th century, followed by Neapolitan rule when it became part of the Kingdom of Naples in 1185. Venetian rule followed in the 15th century, a time of progress for the island. The French, Russians and British all left their legacy on Zákynthos until, in 1953, it was all but destroyed in a mighty earthquake. Zákynthos Town has now been rebuilt in keeping with its original architecture.

TOP 10 ZÁKYNTHOS'S HISTORY

1 **Before 459 BC**
Arkesios of Kefaloniá and Odysseus of Ithaki rule

2 **c.459–446 BC**
Alliance with Athens in First Peloponnesian War

3 **c.700–1185**
The Ionian Islands came under Byzantine rule

4 **1185–1479**
Zákynthos becomes part of the Kingdom of Naples

5 **1479–1797**
Venice rules the island

6 **1797–8**
Briefly part of the French department of Mer-Égée

7 **1798–1807**
Part of Ottoman Empire, in alliance with Russia

8 **1809–64**
After brief French rule, the British take control

9 **1864–present**
The Ionian Islands form a union with Greece

10 **1953**
Major earthquake, after which the towns are rebuilt

Huge cracks in the ground opened up following the catastrophic 1953 earthquake in Zákynthos.

The Top 10 of Everything

The Blue Caves of Zákynthos,
a spectacular natural wonder

📖10 Moments in History

① Colonization by Mainland Greeks (700–500 BC)

Settlers from mainland Greece arrived on the Ionian islands around the mid-8th century BC, but almost no traces of their settlements survive except for the archaeological finds on display in museums. In later centuries, the powerful mainland state of Corinth sent settlers to set up a vassal colony, Corcyra, on Corfu.

Drawing of the battle of Aegospotami

② Peloponnesian War (431–404 BC)

In 436 BC, Corcyra, by then a power to be reckoned with, was drawn into a war between democratic and aristocratic factions in Epidamnus, a smaller city founded by Corcyra on the mainland. Corinth was drawn into the conflict, which soon sucked in Sparta and Corinth's Peloponnesian League allies on one side and Greece's rival superpower, Athens, on the other. The ensuing Peloponnesian War raged across the Hellenic world for a generation, ending only with the defeat of Athens in 404 BC.

③ Subjugation by Rome (197 BC)

The Ionian Islands were a part of the Macedonian empire from the 4th century BC until 197 BC, when Greece was subjugated by Rome. The islands enjoyed peace as part of the Roman Empire until Venetian occupiers arrived in 1204, after the invasion of Constantinople in the Fourth Crusade.

④ Venetian Rule (1204–1797)

The Republic of Venice took control of the Ionians from 1204. This was a key period in the history of the islands – it was due to Venetian fortifications that they avoided occupation during the Ottoman invasion of Greece. As a result, the islands remained Christian.

⑤ The Septinsular Republic and French Occupation (1800–14)

Between 1800 and 1814, the Ionian Islands changed hands three times. When Napoleon conquered Venice in 1797, the islands came with it, only to be taken over the following year by the Russo-Ottoman Septinsular Republic. In 1807, France reclaimed the islands and held them until the collapse of Napoleon's Empire.

⑥ British Protectorate (1814–64)

The 1815 Treaty of Paris placed the Ionian Islands under British protection. During this time the British High Commissioner and an elected assembly worked together to improve the islands' infrastructure.

French leader Napoleon Bonaparte

7 Union with Greece (1864)

Ionian residents wanted a union with Greece after the country gained its independence in 1830. Britain eventually agreed to relinquish the islands, and the Ionians became provinces of the Kingdom of Greece in 1864.

8 Axis Occupation (1941)

During World War II, the Axis alliance, which included Germany, Japan and Italy, took control of Greece. Italy claimed sole power in 1941, but the Germans evicted them in 1943 and killed most of the Jewish population.

Earthquake ruins in Zákynthos, 1953

9 Major Earthquake (1953)

The most significant event in the recent history of the Ionian Islands was the devastating earthquake of 1953. It recorded 7.2 on the Richter scale and destroyed entire towns on Zákynthos and Kefaloniá. Many towns have since been rebuilt to earthquake-proof standards.

10 National Marine Park of Zakynthos (1999)

The National Marine Park protects the island's flourishing marine ecosystem and is home to terrestrial and coastal flora, fauna and avian life. Its founding marks a significant step towards increasing environmental awareness and developing sustainable tourism in Greece.

TOP 10 HISTORICAL FIGURES

Empress Elisabeth of Austria

1 Nikolaos Doxaras
Doxaras (1706–75), a prominent painter whose work combined Byzantine and Italian influences, spent most of his life on Zákynthos.

2 Sir Thomas Maitland
Sir Thomas (1759–1824) was the first British Lord High Commissioner of the Ionians, from 1815 to 1823.

3 Ioannis Capodistrias
Born in Corfu, Capodistrias (1776–1831) led Greece to independence and was the Greek Republic's first premier.

4 Sir Frederick Adam
Sir Frederick (1781–1853) was the second Lord High Commissioner of the Ionians, from 1824 to 1831.

5 Dionýsios Solomós
Zákynthos-born poet Dionýsios Solomós (1798–1857) wrote the Greek national anthem.

6 Empress Elisabeth of Austria
Empress of Bavaria and later of Austria, Elisabeth (1837–98) had Corfu's Achílleion Palace built in the 1890s.

7 King George I
King George I of Greece (1845–1913) used Corfu's Mon Repos Estate as his summer residence.

8 Kaiser Wilhelm II
The last German emperor, Wilhelm II (1859–1941), bought the Achílleion Palace after Elisabeth of Austria died.

9 Ioannis Metaxas
Born in Ithaki, Metaxas (1871–1941) ruled as a dictator of Greece from 1936 until his death.

10 Aristotle Onassis
Billionaire ship-owner Onassis (1906–75), once the richest man in Greece, bought tiny Skorpios, off Lefkada, as a private hideaway. He is buried there.

Myths and Legends

(1) The Odyssey, Ithaki
According to legend, Ithaki was the home of the ancient Greek hero Odysseus, who was depicted so vividly in Homer's epic poem *The Odyssey*. The great warrior returned here from Troy to be reunited with his love, Penelope.

(2) Corinthians, Lefkáda
In ancient times, a narrow strip of land connected Lefkáda to the mainland. Legend has it that the Corinthians, who had established Leukas city – modern-day Lefkáda Town – wanted complete control of the territory, so they destroyed the isthmus to create the island of Lefkáda.

Odysseus statue, Ithaki port

(3) The Nymph Korkyra, Corfu
When Poseidon saw a beautiful water nymph, he was utterly smitten. He abducted and brought her to this magical island, giving it her name, *Kerkyra* or *Korkyra* in Greek. The name is said to be connected to the Byzantine word *Koryfo* (peaks).

(4) Artemis and Apollo, Zákynthos
The divine siblings Artemis and Apollo were said to be particularly fond of Zákynthos. Artemis, goddess of the hunt, loved wandering through the lush woods full of fauna, while Apollo played his lyra under the trees in order to enchant the island and make it more beautiful.

(5) Analipsi Spring, Corfu
Local legend says that visitors who drink from the Analipsi spring, near the highest point of the Kanoni peninsula in southern Corfu, will never return home.

(6) Poseidon, Paxí
Legend has it that Paxí was joined to Corfu in the past, but was separated when the sea god Poseidon (Neptune) became enraged and dealt a blow to the region with his trident. The single island split to become two, so the story goes, and now the island of Paxí lies to the south of Corfu.

Neptune's Horses (1893), an oil painting by Walter Crane

7 The Gorgon Medusa, Corfu

Envious of her beauty, the goddess Athena turned the maiden Medusa into a snake-haired monster whose gaze turned the beholder into stone. Her hideous effigy, carved on the marble pediment of the Temple of Artemis, is the most important exhibit in the collection of the Corfu Archaeological Museum (see p42).

8 Sappho, Lefkáda

Greek poet Sappho was born around 620 BC. It is said that she fell in love with an ugly boatman, Phaon, whom the goddess Aphrodite changed into a handsome man. Phaon rejected Sappho, who then jumped to her death from the cliffs near Cape Lefkáda.

***Sappho and Phaon** (1809), an oil painting by Jacques-Louis David*

9 Panagia Langouvarda, Kefaloniá

Local legend claims that thousands of harmless snakes appear each August at the convent of Panagia Langouvarda, where the Virgin turned the nuns into snakes to save them from a band of pirates. If the snakes do not appear, it is an ill omen, which villagers avert by delivering them by the sackful at the Feast of the Virgin.

10 Nymph Melissanthi, Kefaloniá

The famous blue cave of Kefaloniá is named after the nymph Melissanthi, who is said to have drowned herself here for the love of the god Pan.

TOP 10 HISTORIC SITES

Palaio Frourio fortress, Corfu Town

1 Palaio Frourio, Corfu
This old fortress dominates Corfu Town's skyline (see pp14–15).

2 St Kerkyra Basilica, Corfu
Now lying in ruins, this church was an important place of worship in the 5th century AD (see p17).

3 Mazarakata Mycenean Cemetery, Kefaloniá
An ancient Mycenaean graveyard has been unearthed near Argostolí (see p86).

4 Doric Temple of Kardaki, Corfu
MAP D4 ▪ Corfu Town, Corfu
A 6th-century BC Doric Temple on the Mon Repos Estate (see p17).

5 Angelokastro, Corfu
MAP B3 ▪ Krini, Corfu
Located near Krini, this was the site of the 13th-century Angelokastro fortress.

6 Skála, Kefaloniá
A 3rd-century-BC Roman villa near the town of Skála houses some remarkably well-preserved floor mosaics (see p86).

7 Palaeochóra, Ithaki
MAP J4 ▪ Palaeochóra, Ithaki
Once Ithaki's capital, this medieval site includes ruins of houses and churches.

8 Hypapanti, Paxí
MAP A5 ▪ Hypapanti, Paxí
Legend has it that this sea cave was a Byzantine church dedicated to the Presentation of Christ in the Temple.

9 Cavo Nira Sanctuary, Lefkáda
According to Greek folklore, this ancient sanctuary was once the shrine of Apollo Leukatas (see p76).

10 Monastery of the Revealed Saints, Kefaloniá
MAP H5 ▪ Sámi, Kefaloniá
This ruined monastery retains some important post-Byzantine wall frescoes.

🔟 Museums and Galleries

Fresco from St Andrea's Monastery at the Byzantine Museum, Zákynthos

① Byzantine Museum, Zákynthos

The museum has a fabulous collection of ecclesiastical art comprising pieces that were saved from the island's churches and monasteries following the devastating 1953 earthquake. Displays include icons, paintings, *templons* (sanctuary screens) and even a model of the elegant pre-earthquake town *(see pp34–5)*.

② Antivouniotissa Museum, Corfu

Located in the Church of Panagia Antivouniotissa, one of the oldest churches on the Ionians, this museum has a fabulous collection of Byzantine and post-Byzantine treasures and ecclesiastical artifacts from the 15th to the 20th century *(see p12)*.

③ Museum of Palaiopolis, Mon Repos, Corfu

Exhibitions on life on the island of Corfu in ancient times are the highlights of this museum. The history of the villa housing the museum, Mon Repos *(see p16)*, is also on show, including displays of archaeological excavations held on the estate.

④ Archaeological Museum, Corfu

MAP D3 ▪ Vrela Armeni 1 ▪ 26610 30680 ▪ Open summer: 8am–8pm Wed–Mon; winter: 8:30am–3:30pm daily

The sculptured Gorgon Medusa frieze, found at the ancient site of the Temple of Artemis and dating back to 590 BC, is a highlight here. The 7th-century BC Lion of Menecrates sculpture is also on display.

⑤ Vathý Archaeological Museum, Ithaki

MAP J4 ▪ Vathý, Ithaki ▪ 26740 32200 ▪ Closed temporarily; call ahead

View ceramic pots and vases, metal tools and household items from the Geometric period of Greek art (9th to 7th centuries BC) to Roman times. Many were found during digs at Piso Aetós *(see p87)*. A notable exhibit is a vase with inscriptions about the goddesses Athena and Hera.

⑥ Museum of Asiatic Art, Corfu

Housed in the Palace of St Michael and St George, this museum has over 11,000 pieces of Chinese, Korean and Japanese weapons, furniture and ceramics collected by Corfiot diplomat Grigórios Mános *(see p12)*.

Exhibit from the Museum of Asiatic Art

7 Pantazis Kontomixis Ethnological Museum, Lefkáda

The exhibits in this museum chronicle everyday life on the island. On display are textiles, household items and tools. One room has been transformed to resemble a traditional home, giving a further insight into the island's culture (see pp24–5).

8 Archaeological Museum, Lefkáda

With a collection of artifacts dating from the early Bronze Age, this museum explores Lefkáda's ancient history. Its exhibits were excavated from sites around the island (see p25).

Archaelogical Museum, Lefkáda

9 Museum of Solomós, Zákynthos

Dedicated to famous Zákynthians, including the 19th-century poets Dionýsios Solomós, who wrote the Greek National Anthem, and Andreas Kalvos, this museum has a fine collection of manuscripts and displays of personal possessions. It also houses the tomb of Solomós (see pp32–3).

10 Stavrós Archaeological Museum, Ithaki

MAP H4 ▪ Stavrós, Ithaki ▪ 26740 23955 ▪ Open 8am–4pm Wed–Mon

This compact museum, housed in a single room of a beautiful old village house, has some fantastic exhibits including items believed to date from ancient times, when the nearby Bay of Polis (see p88) was a major port.

TOP 10 UNIQUE MUSEUMS

1 Phonograph Museum, Lefkáda
A stunning private collection of old records and phonographs (see p25).

2 Banknote Museum, Corfu
MAP P5 ▪ Nikiforou Theotoki 32
Corfu's historic banknotes are displayed in this fascinating museum.

3 Casa Parlante, Corfu
MAP P5 ▪ Nikiforou Theotoki 16
▪ 26610 49190
Nineteenth-century Corfu in all its elegant detail comes to life here.

4 Grigorios Xenopoulos Museum, Zákynthos
MAP M2 ▪ Gaita, Zákynthos Town
▪ 26950 45078
The Zákynthian writer's childhood home displays his books and family heirlooms.

5 Monastery of Faneroménis Museum, Lefkáda
Christian art is displayed here (see p24).

6 Karya Museum, Lefkáda
MAP H2 ▪ Kariá, Lefkáda ▪ 26450 41590
Exhibits here showcase the way of life of Lefkádite mountain villagers.

7 Folk Museum, Paxí
MAP B5 ▪ Gäios, Paxí ▪ 26620 32566
Each room here describes Paxi's history.

8 Shell Museum, Corfu
MAP D4 ▪ Benítses Harbour
▪ 26610 72227
Thousands of shells are exhibited here.

9 Maritime Museum, Zákynthos
MAP L2 ▪ Tsiliví
This museum displays a wide range of unique maritime objects.

10 Patounis Soap Factory, Corfu
MAP P2 ▪ Corfu Town ▪ 26610 39806
See olive oil soap being made and stamped in the traditional way here.

Inside the Patounis Soap Factory

🔟 Cathedrals and Monasteries

Katharon Monastery interior, Ithaki

① Katharon Monastery, Ithaki

MAP H4 ■ Anogi, Ithaki

Sitting at an altitude of around 600 m (2,000 ft), Katharon is one of the highest monasteries on the islands. It lies on Mount Niritos, not far from the small village of Anogi. Remote and beautiful, the monastery is dedicated to the Virgin Mary.

② Cathedral of the Evangelistria, Kefaloniá

MAP G5 ■ Argostóli, Kefaloniá

A relatively new landmark in Kefalonia's capital, Argostóli, the Cathedral of the Evangelistria is an enchanting Greek Orthodox structure that was built in 1957. It is significant because of its intricate icons and ico-nostasis, which are the work of cele-brated local artist Theodoroi Poulakis.

③ Platytera Monastery, Corfu

MAP N2 ■ Corfu Town, Corfu

Famous for housing the tomb of the first Governor of Greece – the Corfiot Ioánnis Kapodístrias who held office from 1827 to 1831 – this monastery dates from the 18th century. Nearby there is a statue of the governor.

④ Cathedral of the Virgin, Ithaki

MAP J4 ■ Vathý, Ithaki

Dedicated to the Virgin Mary, this Greek Orthodox cathedral is quite beautiful. Its carved stonework and bell tower, which date from 1820, are well preserved, and the 18th-century iconostasis is one of the finest examples in the Ionians.

⑤ Monastery of the Virgin Hodegetria, Lefkáda

MAP J1 ■ Lefkáda Town outskirts, Lefkáda

Built in 1420, this monastery is the oldest on Lefkáda and is noted for its traditional 15th-century design, characterized by a single aisle and an austere exterior. The craftsmanship of its timber roof is mesmerizing.

⑥ Monastery of the Virgin of Vlacherna, Corfu

MAP D4 ■ Kanóni, Corfu

Set in a stunning location on the islet of Vlacherna and linked to Corfu by a small bridge, the Monastery of the Virgin of Vlacherna dates back cen-turies. The distinctive white building lies on the edge of a beautiful lagoon known as Chalikopoulos.

Monastery of the Virgin of Vlacherna, Corfu

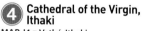

7 Monastery of St John of Lagada, Zákynthos

MAP L2 ■ Katastári, Zákynthos

Mountains provide an impressive backdrop to this remote monastery, which has a delightful chapel with an iconostasis and wall frescoes.

8 Cathedral of the Virgin Spiliotissa, Corfu

MAP P4 ■ Corfu Town, Corfu

Dedicated to one of the island's saints, St Theodora, this Greek Orthodox cathedral in Corfu Town dates from the 16th century. Its carved-wood iconostasis is well-preserved and covered with icons of the Virgin.

Cathedral of the Virgin Spiliotissa

9 Monastery of the Virgin Anafonítria, Zákynthos

MAP K2 ■ Anafonítria, Zákynthos

Home to St Dionýsios from the 16th to 17th centuries, this remote monastery is noted for the gold-covered iconostasis and icons in its small chapel.

10 Monastery of St Gerasímos, Kefaloniá

MAP G5 ■ Argostóli, Kefaloniá

Dedicated to Kefaloniá's patron saint, St Gerasímos *(see p40)*, whose remains lie here, this monastery sits in the foothills of Mount Ainos.

TOP 10 RELIGIOUS FESTIVALS

Easter procession in Corfu

1 Epiphany
Jan
Festivities include the blessing of the waters at seafronts around the islands.

2 Shrove Monday
Early Mar
Signalling the start of Lent, Orthodox Shrove Monday is marked with a service.

3 Lent
Mar–Apr
Most Ionians mark this 40-day period by observing abstinence to commemorate Jesus's fasting before Easter.

4 Good Friday and Easter Monday
Mar or Apr
Pretty bombola lights line the routes of all the Easter processions.

5 Easter
Mar or Apr
Easter is a time for families to celebrate with services and a feast.

6 Procession of the Icon of the Sisies Monastery, Kefaloniá
Mar or Apr
A religious procession, where the icon of the Sisies Monastery is carried through the streets, marks Easter Monday.

7 Pentecost
Jun
This marks the descent of the Holy Ghost. Church services and feasts are held.

8 Dormition of the Virgin
15 Aug
Church services take place.

9 Christmas
Dec
Christmas is marked with festivals, prayers and the giving of gifts.

10 Traditional Festivals
Each island's patron saint is celebrated with traditional festivals of dance, music and feasts in village squares.

🔟 Beaches

The long, sandy and secluded Mýlos beach, Lefkáda

1 Xi Beach, Kefaloniá

Famous for its fine red sand, Xi beach *(see p90)* is located opposite Argostóli and south of Lixoúri on the Pallikí peninsula. Rows of parasols provide shade from the sun, and cliffs form a stunning backdrop.

2 Pórto Katsiki Beach, Lefkáda

Located not far from the windsurfer's paradise of Vasilikí *(see p76)*, Lefkáda's Pórto Katsiki beach *(see p76)*, surrounded by lush vegetation and tall cliffs, is considered one of the best bays on the island. This spectacular beach is horseshoe-shaped and has golden sand and interesting rock formations that are fun to explore.

Beautiful Pórto Katsiki beach, Lefkáda

3 Mýlos Beach, Lefkáda

The sandy Mýlos beach *(see p25)*, with its picturesque old stone windmills, is a great place to go if you wish to escape the crowds. It lies near the lively fishing village of Agios Nikitas *(see p78)*, from where you can walk over the headland to the beach or take a boat along the coast.

4 Platýs Gialos and Makrýs Gialos, Kefaloniá

These two beaches *(see p90)* lie side by side at Lassí on Kefaloniá's west coast, south of Argostóli *(see pp26–7)*. Both are long and sandy, with a scattering of rocks. The sea here is especially safe for swimmers, and watersports enthusiasts can be seen water-skiing and windsurfing.

5 Arillas Beach, Corfu

Located on the northwest coast of Corfu, near the town of Agios Stefanos, Arillas beach *(see p68)* is a long stretch of soft sand and is as picturesque as it is quiet. The turquoise sea breaks against several small islands and islets that lie off its shoreline.

6 Voutoumi Beach, Antipaxí

Sandy Voutoumi beach (see p68) lies on the eastern coast of Antipaxí. It is linked to nearby Vrika beach by a pathway that passes by the vineyards and olive and citrus groves that dominate the island's pretty landscape. The beach offers fabulous views of the coastline, and trees here provide shelter from the sun.

7 Antísamos Beach, Kefaloniá

One of several Kefalonián beaches that featured in the 2001 film *Captain Corelli's Mandolin* (see p29), Antísamos (see p90) is a beautiful beach located near the east-coast town of Sámi (see p85). This white shingle beach looks out across the water to Ithaki opposite and is popular with locals. It has a backdrop of hills and forest.

8 Vrika Beach, Antipaxí

One of the most popular beaches on Antipaxí, Vrika (see p68) is characterized by its golden sands and clear turquoise sea. Yachts and motor boats can often be seen anchored a little way off this picture-postcard cove, while their owners take a dip in the warm water.

Vromi Cove, Zákynthos

10 Vromi Cove, Zákynthos

This pretty cove (see p102) on the west coast of Zákynthos is just one of several dotted along this stretch of coastline, including Exo Chora (see p102) and Navagio beach, also known as Shipwreck Bay (see p99). Vromi overlooks a pristine sea and has soft honey-coloured sand.

View of Vrika beach, Antipaxí

9 Gialiskari Beach, Corfu

The idyllic beach of Gialiskari (see p68) is the prettiest in a string of quiet, sandy coves along Corfu's west coast; its neighbours include Ermones, Pélekas (see p67), Myrtiótissa (see p68) and Agios Gordios. The coastline here is dotted with rock formations, and is a popular camping spot.

🔟 Natural Wonders

Awesome interior of Drogaráti Cave

1 Drogaráti Cave, Kefaloniá

This huge and enchanting cave, located at Sámi, is believed to be more than a million years old. Its interiors are covered in stalactites and stalagmites. The Royal Balcony and the Chamber of Exaltation, which boasts such superb acoustics that it is now often used as a venue for operatic performances, are two of the particularly breathtaking features the cave has to offer *(see p31)*.

2 Grava Gardikiou, Corfu
MAP C5 ■ Southwest coast, Corfu

Of all the the cave formations found across the Ionians, Grava Gardikiou is particularly noted for its ancient history. Archaeological finds from the Upper Palaeolithic period, around 20,000 BC, indicate that this rock shelter may have once been a site where hunters gathered.

3 Lake Melissáni, Kefaloniá

Fed by a system of caves *(see pp30–31)*, this underground lake is a mix of sea water and freshwater. The mineral content gives the lake its deep blue colour. It was named after the nymph Melissáni when ancient artifacts showing the god Pan and several nymphs were discovered here.

4 The Spring of Aretousa, Ithaki
MAP J4 ■ S of Vathý, Ithaki

The Spring of Aretousa is believed to be the one described by Homer in *The Odyssey*, where Odysseus met Eumaeus. Whether this is true or not, the ravine-side walk towards the spring is beautiful, if a little challenging for anyone afraid of heights.

5 Blue Caves, Zákynthos

Located at Cape Skinári on the northernmost tip of Zákynthos, the Blue Caves are a delightful sight – the water between the arches of the caves appears to be a vivid bright blue when the sun shines in. Take a boat from Agios Nikólaos village and sail along the coastline for the best views of the caves *(see p97)*.

The Blue Caves of Zákynthos

6 Korissíon Lagoon, Corfu

A massive stretch of water separated from the sea by sand dunes and beaches, this lagoon is a haven for wildlife, such as sandpipers and egrets. The freshwater lake is around 5 km (3 miles) long and surrounded by lush vegetation (see pp20–21).

7 Kastanitha Cave, Paxí

MAP A5 ■ Near Lákka, Paxí

Kastanitha cave is one of Paxí's most striking natural features. Lying on the northwest coast near Lákka, the 180-m- (590-ft-) tall cave is a fabulous sight as you approach it by boat.

8 Small Islands

More than 30 small islands lie off the coastlines of the main islands of this region. Most of these are rocky and bare, but some have scenic villages and beaches. Vidos, in Corfu's harbour, and Dia (see p88), off Kefaloniá's south coast, are two of the prettiest. The largest is Meganísi (see p77), off Lefkáda's east coast.

9 Katavothres Tunnel, Kefaloniá

MAP G5 ■ Katavothres, Kefaloniá

Sea water disappears underground via this natural tunnel near Argostóli and then makes its way through an elaborate subterranean cave system across the island to Lake Melissáni (see pp30–31). The tunnel was first discovered in the 1950s when experiments were conducted using dye mixed with the lake's water.

Road winding up Mount Pantokrátor

10 Mount Pantokrátor, Corfu

Mount Pantokrátor, whose name means "the Almighty", dominates northeast Corfu. It rises so steeply that its peak, at over 900 m (3,000 ft), is less than 3 km (2 miles) away from the coast. A mountain road with a series of hairpin bends leads to its summit, which affords spectacular views in every direction (see p64).

🔟 Trips to the Mainland

Colourful houses on Párga's seafront

1 Párga
Ionian Cruises, 4 Ethniki Antistaseos, Corfu Town ▪ 26610 38690 ▪ www.ionian-cruises.com

An 80-minute boat trip from Paxí, the pretty harbour town of Párga has two small beaches. Some 37 km (23 miles) to its south is the gate-way to the underworld of Greek legend, the Necromanteaion of Efyra, at the mouth of the River Acheron – known in ancient times as the Styx.

2 Albania
Ionian Cruises, 4 Ethniki Antistaseos, Corfu Town ▪ 26610 38690 ▪ www.ionian-cruises.com

Boats from Corfu Town take around 90 minutes to reach the traditional harbour village of Himare or the larger port of Saranda in Albania. From here, visitors can head to the ruins of ancient Vouthrota (Butrint), a UNESCO World Heritage Site.

3 Chlemoutsi
Ionian Group: www.ionian group.com

An 80-minute boat ride from Poros on Kefaloniá or from Zákinthos Town takes you to this remarkable strong-hold built between 1219 and 1223 on a hilltop 6 km (4 miles) south of the small port of Kyllíni. There are breathtaking views from its ramparts.

4 Dodoni
85 km (52 miles) from Igoumenitsa ▪ Ferries from Corfu Town to Igoumenitsa: www.gtp.gr

More than 3,000 years old, the Oracle of Zeus and the 17,000-seat theatre at Dodoni, on the green slopes of Mount Tomarus, is one of Greece's most impressive ancient sites, but has surprisingly few visitors. It is just over 2 hours' drive from Igoumenitsa.

5 Ancient Olympia
60 km (37 miles) southeast of Kyllíni ▪ Ferries to Kyllíni from Poros on Kefaloniá with Kefalonian Lines: www.kefalonianlines.com; from Zákynthos Town with Ionian Group: www.ioniangroup.com

The birthplace of the Olympic Games is one of Greece's most evocative archaeological sites. The on-site museum has a rich collection of finds from excavations, including ancient arms and armour, marble and terra-cotta statues, ceramics and bronzes.

Temple of Zeus, Olympia

6 Ioánnina
85 km (52 miles) from Igoumenitsa ■ Ferries from Corfu Town to Igoumenitsa: www.gtp.gr

A 2-hour drive from Igoumenitsa, and picturesquely located beside Lake Pamvotis, the city of Ioánnina has a rich architectural heritage. Landmarks include the 17th-century Aslan Pasha Mosque and a formidable Byzantine citadel. The small island of Nisi, in the lake, is dotted with historic churches. Waterside restaurants in its single village serve fresh trout, river crabs and crayfish.

7 Vikos Gorge
110 km (71 miles) from Igoumenitsa ■ Ferries from Corfu Town to Igoumenitsa: www.gtp.gr

Cutting through the Vikos-Aoos National Park, the Vikos Gorge has Greece's most spectacular hiking trail. A 4-km (2-mile) walk can be made between the villages of Mikro Papigko and Vikos. Hiking the full 14-km (9-mile) waymarked trail from Monodendri to Megalo Papigko takes 6–7 hours, so an overnight stay is required.

Ancient Roman mosaic at Nikopolis

8 Nikopolis
40 km (25 miles) from Lefkáda Town ■ www.visit-preveza.com

Founded by the Roman Emperor Octavian (later known as Augustus) to mark his victory over Mark Anthony and Cleopatra at nearby Actium, Nikopolis, surrounded by arched brick walls, is a remarkable relic of the Roman Empire. An excellent museum displays finds from the site, including notable mosaics.

9 Nafpaktos
95 km (60 miles) from Astakós ■ Ferries from Kefaloniá and Ithaki to Astakós: www.gtp.gr

The medieval harbour town of Nafpaktos is surrounded by Venetian ramparts and has a picturesque Venetian port and castle, and a long beach. Named Lepanto by the Venetians, it is famous for the naval battle of Lepanto, which was fought just offshore in 1571.

10 Mesolóngi
48 km (30 miles) from Astakós, 50 km (31 miles) from Pátra ■ Ferries from Kefaloniá and Ithaki to Astakós and Pátra: www.gtp.gr ■ www.greecebirdtours.com

A 90-minute drive from Pátra or Astakós, Mesolóngi played a heroic part in the War of Independence. Lord Byron (1788–1824), romantic poet and champion of the Greek struggle, died here. His heart is buried in the town's Garden of Heroes. Mesolóngi is surrounded by the lagoons and saltpans of the Mesolóngi Lagoon National Park, which attract pelicans, storks and other migrant birds, making it a delight for bird-watchers.

📻 **Children's Attractions**

A Caribbean-themed play area in Corfu's Aqualand water park

① Aqualand, Corfu
MAP C3 ■ Aqualand, Corfu
■ 26610 58351 ■ Open May–Oct:
10am–6pm daily ■ Adm ■ www.
aqualand-corfu.com
Covering more than 8 ha (19 acres),
Aqualand is an amazing collection of
water rides, giant slides and other
water-based attractions. Restaurants,
changing rooms and relaxation areas
for adults are also available.

② Wildlife Walk, Corfu
MAP B1 ■ Sidári, Corfu
■ 26610 37637
This popular attraction in Corfu's
north-coast resort of Sidári is ideal
for the energetic or those who simply
want a break from sunbathing. A
well-marked route runs alongside
a river and over bridges.

③ Bowl 'm Over, Zákynthos
MAP L2 ■ Tsiliví, Zákynthos
■ 26950 25142 ■ Open 11am–late
daily ■ Adm ■ www.bowlmover.gr
With four bowling lanes, pool, foosball
and air-hockey tables, and a children's
play area, this is a great place to have
some holiday fun with the family.
Snacks and drinks can be enjoyed
on the terrace or in the gardens.

**④ Luna Fun Park,
Zákynthos**
MAP L2 ■ Tsiliví, Zákynthos ■ 26950
48035 ■ Open 10am–late daily ■ Adm
■ www.lunafunpark.com
A children's playground with a bouncy
castle, a climbing tower, slides and a
laser arena are just some of the
attractions here. A babysitting service
and refreshments are also available.

**⑤ Fantasy Mini Golf,
Zákynthos**
MAP L2 ■ Tsiliví, Zákynthos ■ 26950
44543 ■ Open 10am–late daily ■ Adm
■ www.fantasyminigolf.com
This fun complex has greens that run
through gardens and past waterfalls
and other attractions. Facilities include
cafés, a bar and a children's play area.

**⑥ Captain Makis Sun
Cruises Glass-Bottom
Boat, Kefaloniá**
MAP G6 ■ Port of Argostóli, Kefaloniá
■ 26710 25775 ■ Adm ■ www.captain
makis.gr
This glass-bottom boat sails to Agios
Nicholas island to see an ancient
shipwreck, and on to the uninhabited
Vardiani island before stopping
ashore at Xi beach for a barbecue.

7 Marathonisi, Zákynthos

MAP M3 ▪ Zákynthos

Boat trips from around Zákynthos take visitors to Marathonisi, an islet within the National Marine Park. It is also called Turtle Island, and here, children have a chance to see the endangered loggerhead sea turtles.

8 Corfu Donkey Rescue, Corfu

MAP B2 ▪ near Doukades village ▪ 06947 375992 ▪ Open 10am–4pm daily ▪ www.corfu-donkeys.com

This refuge provides shelter, food and healthcare to old, sick or abandoned donkeys. Children will love meeting and going for a walk with the animals (they are not permitted to ride them).

9 Odysseia Pirate Ship Boat Tour, Lefkáda

MAP J2 ▪ Nydrí Harbour, Lefkáda ▪ 69323 10975 ▪ Open 6pm–midnight daily ▪ Adm ▪ www.odysseia-lefkada.eu

The Odysseia tour around Lefkáda island includes a visit to Papanikolis sea cave, where you can have a swim, and the islands of Meganísi and Skorpidi, where kids will love the beach barbecue and snorkelling.

The pirate ship Odysseia, Lefkáda

10 Hydropolis, Corfu

MAP C1 ▪ Acharávi, Corfu ▪ 26630 64000 ▪ Open 10am–6pm daily ▪ Adm (special rates after 4pm) ▪ www.gelinavillage.gr

Set in a large estate of landscaped gardens in northern Corfu, Hydropolis combines a sports and leisure centre with numerous pools, giant slides and mini versions of both for children.

TOP 10 FAMILY RESTAURANTS

Terrace dining at Taka Taka, Paxí

1 Taka Taka, Paxí
This friendly restaurant has space for pushchairs and offers a fabulous menu of grilled fish and meat (see p73).

2 Panorama, Corfu
Family owned and run, this restaurant at Perouládes has several menu options for children (see p71).

3 Four Seasons Café, Paxí
This café-restaurant caters for a young clientele with freshly baked homemade pizzas (see p72).

4 Village Taverna, Corfu
Here children can enjoy Greek dishes on an outside terrace (see p71).

5 Basilico, Lefkáda
Located on the waterfront at Nydrí, Basilico is famous for its popular children's menu, which features Greek dishes and delicious desserts (see p81).

6 Trata Taverna, Lefkáda
MAP J2 ▪ Nydrí, Lefkáda ▪ 26450 92690 ▪ €€
Children love this taverna's superb food, which is cooked on a griddle.

7 The Pines Restaurant, Kefaloniá
Children are sure to find a dish they like from the wide selection of meze dishes offered here (see p95).

8 Sirens Restaurant, Ithaki
International and traditional Greek dishes are served at this family-friendly nautical-themed restaurant (see p95).

9 Mouria Restaurant, Zákynthos
MAP M3 ▪ Laganas, Zákynthos ▪ 26950 51113 ▪ €€
Children will enjoy the tasty dishes on offer at this beachside restaurant.

10 Flocas Café, Zákynthos
A menu for young appetites makes this Argási café a family favourite (see p105).

🔟 Restaurants

Colourful dining terrace at Tassia, Kefalonía

1 Ambelonas, Corfu
Set in an estate in the middle of a beautiful vineyard that has been producing wine and olive oil for over 400 years, this restaurant offers a wide-ranging menu of traditional Corfiot dishes, paired with fine wines from the estate. It also offers cooking classes and has an Olive Oil and Wine Museum (see p71).

2 Elli's, Kefaloniá
Located alongside the pebble beach at Fiskárdo harbour, Elli's is an elegant restaurant within the stone walls of an old Venetian merchant's house. With a classic Mediterranean menu, it is bursting with gorgeous fish and seafood dishes, and vegetarian fare. Elli's is a favourite with locals, especially those celebrating an occasion (see p95).

3 Fryni Sto Mólos, Lefkáda
One of the best meze spots in town, Fryni Sto Mólos specializes in the Greek tradition of serving several small dishes at once. Expect to have *keftedes* (meatballs), souvlaki and a host of dips, such as tzatziki and taramasalata brought to your table. The beer and wine here are also excellent (see p80).

4 Zolithros, Lefkáda
A classic blue and white Greek taverna with an alfresco dining terrace right on the harbourside in Mikros Gïalos, Zolithros specializes in the freshest of fish dishes. You can choose your fish, which is almost certainly caught that very morning by the taverna's owner, before it is cooked with herbs and spices on the barbecue (see p80).

5 Tassia, Kefaloniá
Located by the harbour in Fiskárdo, the acclaimed Tassia serves great seafood dishes, pastas and salads, and its wine list is excellent. Run by chef and cookbook author Tassia Dendrinou, it's a great place at which to relax over a meal (see p95).

6 Essence Restaurant, Zákynthos
Expect à la carte cuisine and fine wines at this stylish restaurant set in a quieter spot outside the centre of Kalamáki. Daily tapas dishes, along with its consistently popular meze platters, add to the menu choices. Essence has a trendy chic decor and a welcoming ambience (see p105).

7 Captain Spiros Taverna, Antipaxos

The perfect place to taste traditional Greek cuisine and beautifully prepared fresh seafood. Captain Spiros Taverna also has vegan options, excellent wines and great service. It is set in an idyllic location on the Vrika Beach, and offers great views of the turquoise waters of the Ionian sea (see p71).

8 Zakanthi Restaurant, Zákynthos

The atmosphere of this charming restaurant in the centre of Kalamáki will have you returning time and again. Sit in the lush garden full of shrubs – it looks particularly enchanting after dark when all the lights are lit. The delicious food, comprising mainly grills and salads, is served in generous portions (see p105).

9 Sirens Restaurant, Ithaki

One of island's best restaurants, Sirens is run by Marina Fotopoulos, who specializes in Ithakan cuisine. It offers international favourites as well as local dishes, such as a delicious claypot of lamb and potatoes and Ithakan tomato and feta cheese omelette. Maritime memorabilia adorns the walls (see p95).

10 Poseidon Fish Tavern, Itakí

Housed in a gorgeous whitewashed merchant's house just off Vathý harbour, Poseidon serves freshly caught fish and seafood, including octopus, lobster and swordfish, along with homemade pies and meats cooked on charcoal. Each dish is plated with considerable artistic flair (see p95).

Souvlaki dish at Poseidon Fish

TOP 10 MEZE DISHES

Dolmades, a popular meze

1 Dolmades
A distinctive Greek dish, dolmades are made by stuffing vine leafs with aromatic rice and ground meat.

2 Taramasalata
A sumptuous dip that is light pink or white in colour, taramasalata is made from cod's roe and breadcrumbs.

3 Tahini
A mixture of ground sesame seeds and garlic laced with lemon juice, this dip goes well with salad.

4 Kreatópita
A Kefalonián delicacy, these small pies are stuffed with a mouthwatering mixture of meat and local herbs.

5 Choriátiki Saláta
An appetizing blend of tomatoes, cucumber, peppers and olives, topped with feta cheese and basil.

6 Souvlaki
A small kebab of diced pork or lamb on skewers, served chargrilled with lemon and herbs, souvlaki is one of the most popular Greek dishes.

7 Revithosaláta
Sometimes also known as hummus, revithosaláta is a Greek dip made with chickpeas, garlic and coriander.

8 Melitzanosalata
Aubergines are cooked and pureed with tomatoes, garlic and lemon to create this tasty dip.

9 Tzatziki
A refreshing dip made from natural yogurt, diced cucumber and garlic, this goes well with just about every dish.

10 Skordaliá
A dip or sauce of the Ionians, skordaliá is made from a mixture of mashed potato, garlic and lemon.

🔟 Corfu and the Ionian Islands for Free

Arts and crafts shop, Corfu Old Town

1 Arts and Crafts

It's worth looking out for posters advertising local arts and crafts markets, which are often held around the islands' harbours on one Sunday a month. You'll find plenty of art galleries and shops too, where you're almost certain to find some-thing to purchase and take home as a souvenir. If you're in Sámi, Kefaloniá, seek out IN Gallery and Annikas Greek Handicrafts (see p92).

2 Admire a sunset

No visit to the Ionian Islands would be complete without seeing one of its legendary sunsets. The beaches at Pélekas on Corfu and Kerí on Zákynthos are two of the best spots to enjoy a spectacular view.

Sunset view from Zákynthos

3 Special Events

Mingle with the locals to watch Corfu's Achílleion Marathon. This annual summer event begins with a parade through Corfu Old Town, followed by the race itself, and then celebrations featuring performances by musicians, singers and dancers. Similar free events can be found throughout the Ionians.

4 Festivals

The Greek calendar is bursting with annual festivals. Easter is the biggest celebration of the Orthodox church and is a time when all the islands host events, over several days, which bring entire communities together. Watch processions and enjoy free live music (see p45).

5 Museums

The Ionian Islands are home to some fabulous museums, such as the Byzantine Museum in Zákynthos Town (see p32) and Lefkáda Town's Archaeological Museum (see p25). Many have free admission days, such as International Museums Day on 18 May. Most of them also have at least one Sunday a month when you can visit for free.

6 Patron Saints' Days

All the islands mark saints' days and namedays, which are similar to birthdays. In Zákynthos, locals offer celebratory food and wine to visitors to mark their patron saint's day (Agios Dionýsios) on 24 August and 17 December each year.

7 Walking and Hiking

All the islands have tourist offices where you can get free guides with suggested town walks or hiking routes. Some suggestions are leisurely strolls taking in the sights, while others are more challenging and are designed for serious hikers.

8 Carnivals

The islands are famous for their *apokries* (carnival season) and the carnivals often have religious connections. The spring carnival, for instance, takes place three weeks before Lent and features dances with traditional music. It is free to join in and locals, especially children, dress up in elaborate fancy-dress costumes.

Monastery of St Gerasímos, Kefaloniá

9 Visit a Monastery

The Ionian Islands are dotted with monasteries housing fabulous icons and tombs, and most of these are free to visit. Special events are held on their nameday or saint's day, or on days of significance to the monastery. At the Katharon Monastery on Ithaki, for instance, a free feast is held on the eve of 7 September, to mark the day an icon of the Virgin Mary survived a fire undamaged.

10 Old Quarters

Don't miss the chance to explore the old quarters of the islands' capitals. Corfu Old Town and parts of Lefkáda Town are full of history. While some were destroyed by the 1953 earthquake, capitals like Zákynthos Town and Kefaloniá's Argostóli were rebuilt to their original style.

TOP 10 BUDGET TIPS

Local food market, Corfu

1 If you are self-catering, try bulk buying at larger supermarkets rather than at overpriced mini-markets in resorts. For smaller purchases of fresh produce, visit local food markets.

2 Visit the islands in April and May or in October when the weather is pleasant, and flights, accommodation and car rentals are cheaper.

3 Renting a car by the day from a local agency can be cheaper than using taxis.

4 Students, school pupils and senior citizens are entitled to reduced admission at many archaeological sites and museums with proof of status.

5 Prices in restaurants with multi-lingual tourist menus are almost always higher than in those that cater mainly to locals.

6 Local wines "apo to bareli" (from the barrel) are cheaper than bottled vintages. Order by the jug in tavernas, or buy in bottles in local shops.

7 Fish dishes are usually the most expensive on the menu. Squid and *marides* (whitebait) are the cheapest seafood options.

8 Private currency exchange agencies usually claim to charge no commission but offer a poorer rate of exchange than banks or ATMs.

9 Greek beer and spirits are cheaper in bars and shops than imported brands.

10 Almost every resort has at least one happy-hour bar where drinks are half price in the early evening.

🔟 Festivals and Events

Greek dancers performing in traditional costumes

1 Town Carnivals
Feb or Mar

Every town hosts week-long pre-Lenten events that culminate in grand processions of floats at this time. People of all ages, but especially children, don costumes and masks as part of the festivities.

Litany of St Spyrídon procession

2 Litany of St Spyrídon, Corfu
Palm Sun, Holy Sat, 11 Aug & first Sun in Nov

The Litany of St Spyrídon is a religious event and music festival. It honours Corfu's patron saint, St Spyrídon, the Keeper of the City, who is said to have rid Corfu of the plague and protected it from the Turkish invasion.

3 Holy Saturday, Corfu
Mar or Apr

Corfu's Easter celebrations are famous all over Greece, not least for the custom on the morning of Holy Saturday, when residents joyously throw clay vessels out from their balconies as church bells ring.

4 Folklore Festivals
May–Aug

It is the tradition for each village in Greece to host a folklore festival at least once during the year. This is a time when the local residents meet up with friends and neighbours to feast together. Dance troupes also often perform traditional dances that are accompanied by folk bands.

5 Union of the Ionians
21 May

Celebrations to mark the Union of the Ionian Islands with Greece in 1864 (see p39) include traditional dance and music performances, plus many more cultural events. Entire communities gather in village centres to enjoy the entertainment and to feast on local food.

Cultural Festivals
Jul & Aug

Lively festivals of music, dance, theatre, art and literature are held in various towns in the Ionians such as the Kefallonía Theatre Festival, the Music and Theatre Festival (Vathý, Ithaki) and the Festival of Art and Literature (Lefkáda).

7 **Litany of St Gerasímos, Kefaloniá**
16 Aug & 20 Oct

Kefaloniá hosts festivals for its patron saint, the 16th-century St Gerasímos (see p40). St Gerasímos is believed to protect Kefaloniáns from illness.

8 **Ochi Day**
28 Oct

A public holiday, this marks the day when Greek prime minister Ioannis Metaxas rejected Italian dictator Mussolini's ultimatum to allow Axis forces to occupy parts of Greece in 1940. He proclaimed "ochi!" ("no").

Participants in an Ochi Day parade

9 **Saints' Day Festivals**
The naming day of the patron saint of each town is widely celebrated. The annual festivities at this time bring many people back to their homes. Church services are followed by traditional music, dancing and local dishes.

 Wine Festivals
A good wine year is marked in style in the islands, with live music and feasts. Towns hosting events include Fragkáta in Kefaloniá, Perachóri in Ithaki, Moraitika in Corfu, Plános in Zákynthos and Lefkáda Town.

TOP 10 OTHER EVENTS

Carnival celebrations in Corfu

1 Carnival, Corfu Town
Late Feb or early Mar
Locals in fancy costumes parade around the Plateia Spianáda and the Liston.

2 Achílleion Marathon, Corfu
First Sun in Jun
Runners take part in this annual event to raise awareness of sport in Corfu.

3 Backgammon Festival, Zákynthos
End of Jun or early Jul
Enthusiasts attend this annual festival held in early summer each year.

4 Cricket Festival, Corfu Town
Jul & Aug
In a throwback to British rule, this celebrates the Corfiots' love of cricket.

5 Varkarola, Corfu
Aug
This festival celebrates Corfu being saved from Turkish invasion in 1716.

6 Music Festival, Argostóli, Kefaloniá
Aug
Greek and international musicians come together for a series of summer concerts.

7 Wine Festival, Ithakí
Aug
This celebration of a successful grape harvest brings Ithakíans together.

8 Valaoritia Festival, Nydrí, Lefkáda
Aug
This festival honours Lefkádian politician and poet Aristotelis Valaoritis (1824–79).

9 International Folklore Festival, Lefkáda
Aug
A parade and traditional dances are the highlights of this festival.

10 International Music Festival, Paxí
Sep
Greek musicians join the people of Paxí in a celebration of classical music.

Corfu and the Ionian Islands Area by Area

The picturesque waterside village of Kioni on Ithaki island

🔟 Corfu, Paxí and Antipaxí

The lush Islands of Corfu, Paxí and Antipaxí, which lie between the heel of Italy and the western part of mainland Greece, are the northernmost islands in the Ionian archipelago. Corfu, the second largest of the Ionians after Kefaloniá, is a curious mix of old and new. Cosmopolitan resorts, such as Benítses and Sidári, with their modern accommodation, busy bars and watersports facilities, dot the island's pretty coastline, while traditional villages cling to the slopes of Mount Pantokrátor. The historic heart of the island's capital, Corfu Old Town has charming cobbled streets, ancient fortresses and grand palaces. The smaller islands of Paxí and Antipaxí are known for their natural beauty, pretty towns, bays and beaches.

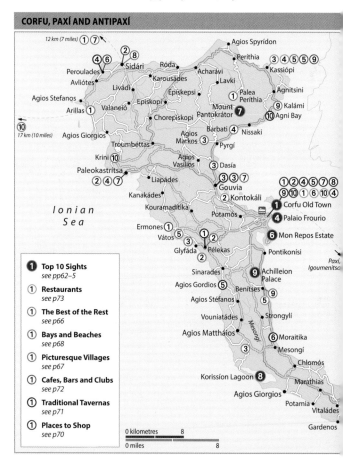

CORFU, PAXÍ AND ANTIPAXÍ

1 Top 10 Sights
see pp62–5

① Restaurants
see p73

① The Best of the Rest
see p66

① Bays and Beaches
see p68

① Picturesque Villages
see p67

① Cafes, Bars and Clubs
see p72

① Traditional Tavernas
see p71

① Places to Shop
see p70

Rooftops of Corfu Old Town

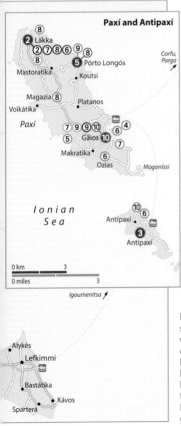

1 Corfu Old Town

Designated a UNESCO World Heritage Site in 2007, Corfu Old Town is a remarkable blend of architectural styles. From the French-style Liston, with its chic cafés and arcaded terraces, to the Venetian buildings around the Plateia Spianáda, and from the imposing Palaio Frourio to the Neo Frourio fortress, the town has something for everyone. Highlights include the atmospheric Church of St Spyrídon and the oldest official building in Greece, the Palace of St Michael and St George (see pp12–13).

2 Lákka, Paxí
MAP A5

Lákka lies to the north of the island, not far from the mysterious sea cave known as Hypapanti (see p41). Nestled in a cove that provides shelter from the strong winds of the open sea, it is a popular sailing and watersports destination. To its west are a series of excellent beaches where the sand is soft and the turquoise waters are safe for swimming.

Voutoumi beach, Antipaxí

3 Antipaxí
MAP B6

Lying to the south of Paxí is the small satellite island of Antipaxí, which has a population of less than 60 permanent inhabitants. A daily boat sails to and from Paxí's Gäios harbour, although most islanders have their own boats and it is possible to rent one in high season. This tiny but picturesque island is a haven of golden beaches and clear waters.

4 Palaio Frourio, Corfu Town

Founded by the Byzantines in the 11th century, this mighty fortress was rebuilt by the Venetians in the 14th century and further expanded by the British in the 19th century. It contains stunning Byzantine, medieval and colonial architecture and treasures, including churches, a museum with Byzantine art, a library and military cannon. There are superb views of Corfu Town and the mainland from its highest point (see pp14–15).

Cannon in Palaio Frourio, Corfu Town

5 Pórto Longós, Paxí
MAP B5

The idyllic harbourside village of Pórto Longós lies on the east coast of Paxí, to the north of Gäios. Here, fishing and leisure boats bob gently in the water, tavernas selling fresh fish line the long horseshoe-shaped bay and charming houses dot the lush terraced landscape.

GERALD DURRELL

When Durrell moved with his family to Corfu as a boy in 1935, he became fascinated by the island's flora and fauna. The start of a life-long love of animals, Durrell's Corfiot years were later recounted in his Corfu Trilogy – *My Family and Other Animals* (1956), *Birds, Beasts, and Relatives* (1969) and *The Garden of the Gods* (1978).

6 Mon Repos Estate, Corfu Town

Created by the second Lord High Commissioner of the Ionian Islands, Sir Frederick Adam, this estate is famous for once being the summer home of the Greek royal family. Within its grounds are the remains of the ancient city of Palaeopolis. Minutes away are the scenic resorts of Kanóni and Pontikonisi (Mouse Island), which are popular spots at which to take photos (see pp16–17).

7 Mount Pantokrátor, Corfu
MAP C2

Dominating the skyline to the north, the 900-m- (3,000-ft-) high Mount Pantokrátor is the tallest mountain on Corfu. While its south-facing slopes are carpeted with olive groves and pine forests, the northern slopes are rugged and barren. From its peak you can see Albania on a clear day.

Pórto Longós' pretty harbour, Paxí

8 **Korissíon Lagoon, Corfu**
Corfu's Korissíon Lagoon is home to several species of wildlife. Egrets and sandpipers, for example, can be seen around the 5-km- (3-mile-) long freshwater lake. Located on the southern coastline of Corfu island, Korissíon Lagoon is separated from the Ionian Sea by a solid stretch of sand dunes and beaches, and can be reached from Mesongí (see pp20–21).

Grand interior of the Achílleion Palace

9 **Achílleion Palace, Corfu**
Located along the coast en route to Benítses, this elegant palace was the whim of Empress Elisabeth of Austria, also known as Sissi, who adored ancient Greek mythology. The palace and grounds are dotted with statues of Apollo, Hera, Achilles and Artemis. After Elisabeth's assassination the palace remained vacant until Kaiser Wilhelm II of Germany bought it in 1907 (see pp18–19).

10 **Gäios, Paxí**
MAP B6
Located on the east coast of Paxí, the small, pretty town of Gäios is the main port and commercial centre of the island. Traditional Greek houses and tavernas line the tiny winding streets and picturesque harbourside here. The harbour is popular with leisure sailors because the water is so calm – an offshore island, Agios Nikólaos (see p66), sits at the harbour entrance acting as a natural breakwater.

A DAY TRIP FROM CORFU TOWN TO PAXÍ

Lákka
Pórto Longós
Corfu Town 60 km (37 miles)
Magazia
Paxí
Ferry boarding point
Gäios
Ozias

▶ MORNING

Start your day by heading to the New Port at **Corfu Old Town** (see p63). **Kamelia Lines** operates ferries and hydrofoils between Corfu and Gäios, on Paxos. The fastest crossing takes 55 minutes. Timetables change monthly, with more frequent departures in June, July and August, so check the ferry information on www. paxos-thalassatravel.com for up-to-date schedules. Once you have disembarked, hire a car for a few hours or take a taxi around the island. Start by heading north along the coastal road to the village of **Pórto Longós**, where you can explore the lively harbourside and enjoy a delicious lunch at **Nionios Taverna** (see p71), one of several excellent restaurants that can be found along the waterfront here.

AFTERNOON

After having lunch, take the road signposted to **Lákka** (see p63). Spend time in the village and on nearby beaches with their clear turquoise water before driving south past the tiny hamlets of **Magazia** and **Ozias** (see p67), on the way back to Gäios. While the distance is less than 10 km (6 miles) and does not take long to drive, it is worth taking your time to stop to admire the great views. Back at Gäios, visit the Venetian square and enjoy a meal at any of the nearby restaurants, such as **Taka Taka** (see p73) or **Taverna Vassilis** (see p71). Afterwards, head to the harbour and hop back on the hydrofoil for the return journey to Corfu.

See map on pp62–3 ←

The Best of the Rest

1 Ereikoússa Island
MAP A1

One of the three satellite islands of Corfu, Ereikoússa, is known for its cypress trees, great beaches and the tiny yet busy town of Pórto. Reach it by boat from Sidári or Corfu Town.

2 Paleokastrítsa, Corfu
MAP B3 ■ West coast, Corfu

This popular resort has three sandy coves, backed by forest, with bright turquoise waters. A monastery sits on a hill, and opposite lie remains of Angelokastro, a 13th-century fortress.

Beautiful Paleokastrítsa bay, Corfu

3 Gardiki Castle, Corfu
MAP C5 ■ Near Skidi village, southwest coast, Corfu

The remains of a 13th-century castle lie on Corfu's southwest coast. This Byzantine fortress was once part of the island's defences.

4 Panagia Islet, Paxí
MAP B5 ■ Off Gäios New Port, Paxí

Panagia islet, or the Island of the Virgin Mary, lies at the entrance to Gäios. Its hilltop basilica and rugged shoreline are best seen from a boat.

5 Kassiópi, Corfu
MAP D1 ■ N of Corfu Town, Corfu

The remains of a Byzantine fortress are located at this small village that has lost none of its old-world charm. It also has a pretty harbour area.

6 Agios Nikólaos Islet, Paxí
MAP B5 ■ Off Gäios New Port, Paxí

Also lying at the entrance to Gäios on Paxí, Agios Nikólaos has two churches and a fort believed to be Byzantine.

7 Mathraki Island
MAP A1

Quiet Mathraki is the smallest of the Diapontians (Corfu's three satellite islands). Tiny communities can be found in Benatika and around Plakes, where boats from Sidári arrive.

8 Sidári, Corfu
MAP B1 ■ Ormos Sidári, Corfu

Sidári can trace its history back to pre-Neolithic times. Today, it's a resort famed for its Canal d'Amour, a natural channel cut out over millennia by the sea. Legend has it that couples who swim through this "Channel of Love" will stay together forever.

9 Benítses, Corfu
MAP D4 ■ S of Corfu Town, Corfu

One of the liveliest tourist spots on the island, this east-coast resort has tavernas and nightspots and offers endless watersports.

10 Othonoí Island
MAP A1

Othonoí, the largest of the Diapontians, is reached by boat from Arillas. It's the place, according to ancient Greek mythology, where a shipwrecked Odysseus met Princess Nausikka, who nursed him back to health.

Kalipso Bay, Othonoí Island

Picturesque Villages

 Palea Períthia
Huddled beneath the peak of Mount Pantokrátor, this is one of the oldest preserved mountain villages on Corfu. The medieval village is also noted for the restored Byzantine frescoes within the 14th-century church of Agios Iákovos O Pérsis.

 Pélekas, Corfu
MAP C4 ■ W of Corfu Town, Corfu
This pretty hamlet offers not only great beaches and tavernas, but also a real sense of community, village folklore and a rich cultural heritage. It is easily reached from Corfu Town.

③ Agios Markos, Corfu
MAP C2 ■ East coast, Corfu
Resting at the foothills of Mount Pantokrátor, this pretty village can be found along the road from coastal Barbati to Ano Korakiana inland. Its picturesque Heptanesian architecture is particularly noteworthy.

④ Barbati, Corfu
MAP C2 ■ East coast, Corfu
Although Barbati is known more for its exquisite and unspoiled 2-km- (1-mile-) long beach, complete with the remains of an ancient church in the shingle, this is one of Corfu's prettiest east-coast villages.

 Vátos, Corfu
MAP B3 ■ West Corfu
The charming village of Vátos in west Corfu is made up of tiny streets and traditional bougainvillea-covered stone houses. It looks out over the glorious west coast beaches of Myrtiótissa and Ermones.

⑥ Ozias, Paxí
MAP B6
Paxí's second-largest community after Gäios, Ozias is the most southerly village on the island. Its harbour has huge boulders through which wind holes have been eroded over time, while nearby are the ruins of an ancient church.

⑦ Gouvia, Corfu
MAP C3 ■ East coast, Corfu
Located on the site of a Venetian harbour and home to Corfu's largest marina, Gouvia is a delightful village with a modern edge. Its traditional stone buildings house chic tavernas.

⑧ Magazia, Paxí
MAP A5
Close to the Stachai caves and, a little further on, the Petriti cave, Magazia is probably best known for its fabulous sunsets. This traditional village lies inland amid olive groves.

 Kalámi, Corfu
MAP D2 ■ Northeast coast, Corfu
Set in a horseshoe-shaped bay, this traditional village was once home to the British author Lawrence Durrell (1912–90). Its pebble beach boasts the prestigious Blue Flag Award.

View of Kalámi's pretty bay, Corfu

⑩ Krini, Corfu
MAP B2 ■ West coast, Corfu
Known for its beautiful location and fabulous sea views, Krini is a traditional Corfiot village that exudes charm. Nearby lie the remains of the Byzantine Angelokastro fortress.

See map on pp62–3

Bays and Beaches

View overlooking Antipaxí's picture-perfect Voutoumi Beach

1 Arillas Beach, Corfu
MAP A2 ■ Near Agios Stefanos, Corfu

Tucked into Corfu's northwestern corner, Arillas is a long and sandy stretch of beautiful beach. You can watch the sea break on the islets that lie just off the shoreline.

2 Gialiskari Beach, Corfu
MAP C4 ■ Near Pélekas, Corfu

Head for this tranquil beach, tucked away in a small cove, if you want some peace and quiet. It is accessible only from Sinarades and few people take the small road down from the town.

3 Myrtiótissa Beach, Corfu
MAP B4 ■ West coast, Corfu

A small, secluded horseshoe-shaped beach, Myrtiótissa is set in a stunning location. With no tavernas and only sheer cliffs and golden sands, it is a favourite with nature-lovers.

4 Paleokastrítsa Beach, Corfu
MAP B3 ■ Ormos Liapádhon, west coast, Corfu

This popular west-coast beach is famous for being a favourite haunt of Sir Frederick Adam (see p17). Tavernas provide shade and refreshments.

5 Agrilas Bay, Paxí
MAP A6 ■ West coast, Paxí

Lying west of Ozias, this bay is one of the largest sweeps of rugged coastline on the west coast. It has a few tiny beaches, including pretty Avlaki beach.

6 Voutoumi Beach, Antipaxí
MAP B6 ■ S of Vrika beach, Antipaxí

Lying just south of the famous Vrika beach is Voutoumi, the other well-known beach on Antipaxí. It is popular due to its turquoise seas and an attractive stretch of sand and pebbles. A walkway links it to Vrika beach.

7 Plakes Beach, Paxí
MAP B5 ■ Near Gäios, Paxí

Located on the outskirts of Gäios, Plakes beach is one of several popular beaches along this stretch of Paxí's coastline. Others include Yanna and Kaki Langada, which is surrounded by rocks.

8 Arkoudaki Beach, Paxí
MAP A5 ■ Near Lákka, Paxí

Accessible only by boat, the small and beautifully secluded Arkoudaki beach is located on the northeastern tip of Paxí. It is a favourite spot for sailors to jump off their yachts.

9 Levrechio Beach, Paxí
MAP B5 ■ East coast, Paxí

This attractive beach lies a little way south of Pórto Longós. It is largely made up of fine shingle, and attracts many visitors in the summer months.

10 Vrika Beach, Antipaxí
MAP B6

Vrika is probably the most famous of Antipaxí's fabulous golden beaches. The journey there takes you through a countryside of vineyards.

Outdoor Activities

 Nature Trails
All the islands have nature trails, but Antipaxí is particularly popular with nature-lovers as it is quite small and easy to navigate. It has a wealth of wildlife, including small mammals and reptiles.

 Sailing
The bays, beaches and coves of Corfu, Paxí and Antipaxí are a delight to explore on a sailing boat. The islands all have harbours where leisure boats can moor.

 Swimming
While some bays are protected, others have strong currents and swimmers should take care. Gently sloping beaches for safe swimming include those at Benítses (see p66) on Corfu and near Gäios (see p65) on Paxí.

Beachcombing
The islands' beaches offer numerous opportunities for beachcombing for items washed ashore, such as driftwood and seashells. Always respect the environment and do not litter the beach.

 Watersports
Major resorts offer plenty of watersports, from scuba diving, water-skiing and windsurfing to banana-boat rides, canoeing and pedalo rides. The resorts that also offer training are Corfu's Sidári, Benítses and Kassiópi (see p66).

Scuba diving off the coast of Corfu

 Olive Picking
Get a taste of island life by joining the olive harvest on Paxí, where there are more than 200,000 olive trees. Harvest starts in early November.

Ermones golf course, Corfu

 Golf
www.corfugolfclub.com
The Corfu Golf Club's 18-hole, par-72 course in Ermones in the Ropa Valley is among the best in Greece.

Horse Riding
www.trailriderscorfu.com, www.kephalonia.com
Trailriders, based at Ano Korakiano on Corfu, organizes rides through olive groves. Bavarian Horse Riding Stables on Kefaloniá also offers delightful rides.

Walking
www.thecorfutrail.com
If you like walking in the open countryside, the islands offer every opportunity for walks along coastal roads or in the rugged inland terrain.

Cycling
All the major tourist resorts offer bicycles for hire. However, unless you are particularly athletic and like rough terrain, it is best to stay on level ground.

See map on pp62–3

Places to Shop

① Land of Corfu Natural Products, Corfu

MAP P5 ■ 25 Filarmonikis, Corfu Town

Artisan soaps and cosmetics made from locally produced argan, cedar, kumquat, olive and prickly pear oils can be bought here. There are also shells and sea sponges.

② Leather Market, Corfu

MAP P5 ■ 7 Dona St, Corfu Town ■ 26610 21297

This market is the place to visit if you want a beautifully handmade leather jacket, handbag, wallet or belt.

Bags at the Maska Leather Workshop

③ Maska Leather Workshop, Corfu

MAP C3 ■ Gouvia Bay, Corfu ■ 26610 90542

This large workshop and store sells a large selection of unusual clothes and handmade leather bags, belts and shoes in a range of colours. The owner can adapt items to suit your preference and size.

④ Muses, Corfu

MAP P1 ■ 22 Michael Theotoki St, Corfu ■ 26610 30708

This inspired concept store with pop-ups in Berlin, Paris and New York unites contemporary design with tradition and true artistry for a range of unique fashion and housewares.

⑤ Antivouniotissa Museum Shop, Corfu

MAP Q1 ■ Palaio Frourio, Corfu Town

The shop at this excellent museum sells high-quality copies of Byzantine and Venetian works of religious art and CDs of Orthodox choral music.

⑥ George Apergis Jewels, Paxi

MAP A5 ■ Lákka ■ 26620 33008

Housed in a yellow-washed cottage, this jewellery shop offers a range of contemporary gold and silver rings, necklaces and bracelets.

⑦ Olive Wood Workshop by Tom

MAP P1 ■ Nikiforou Theotoki, Corfu Old Town ■ 26610 46683

Beautiful wooden bowls, dishes, cases, ornamental boxes, photo-frames and jewellery are made and displayed here.

⑧ Patounis Soap Factory, Corfu

MAP P5 ■ 9 Ioannou Theotokou, Corfu Town

Traditionally made soaps using olive oil from island groves have been produced at this family-run business since 1891. It also runs interesting guided tours around its workshop.

⑨ Icon Gallery, Corfu

MAP P6 ■ 52 Guilford, Corfu Town ■ 26610 400928

A selection of hand-painted copies of saintly Greek Orthodox icons and other works of Greek sacred art by more than 30 skilled local artists are on sale at this small, friendly art gallery. There are also jewellery and ornaments. All the pieces are superbly handcrafted.

⑩ Ilias Lalaounis, Corfu

MAP P5 ■ 35 Kapodistriou, Corfu Town ■ 26610 36258

The Corfu branch of Greece's most exclusive jeweller sells fine gold and silver pieces.

See map on pp62–3

Traditional Tavernas

1 **Ambelonas, Corfu**
Agios Ioannis, Pelekas ▪ 69321 58888 ▪ Open Jun–Nov: 7–11pm Wed–Fri; Dec–May: 1–6pm Sun ▪ €
Sample authentic Corfiot dishes at this lovely taverna amid olive groves in the heart of an age-old estate farm.

2 **Captain Spiros Taverna, Antipaxos**
MAP B6 ▪ Vrika Beach, Antipaxos ▪ 69728 16229 ▪ Open 9am–5pm daily ▪ €€
Nothing is more traditional on the islands than enjoying fresh grilled fish or lobster pasta right by the sea. This idyllic place on Vrika beach has a loyal following.

3 **Vergina, Corfu**
MAP C3 ▪ Gouvia, Corfu ▪ 26610 90093 ▪ €€
This spacious, traditional taverna serves local favourites, such as souvlaki. There is also Greek music and dancing every evening.

4 **Panorama, Corfu**
MAP A1 ▪ Peroulades, Corfu ▪ 26630 95035 ▪ €
Perched high on a cliff on the coast near Sidári, this atmospheric restaurant boasts fantastic sunset views. Meat grills and local fare are served.

5 **Taverna Sebastian, Corfu**
MAP C4 ▪ Agios Gordios, Sinarades, Corfu ▪ 26610 53256 ▪ €€
Established in 1977, this traditional taverna specializes in Corfiot dishes inspired by the staff's own recipes.

PRICE CATEGORIES
For a three-course meal for one with half a bottle of wine (or equivalent meal), taxes and extra charges.

€ under €30   €€ €30–€50   €€€ over €50

6 **Village Taverna, Corfu**
MAP D5 ▪ Moraitika, Corfu ▪ 26610 76403 ▪ Closed Oct–May ▪ €
This taverna has a lovely alfresco terrace and serves classic Greek food, including Corfiot specialities.

7 **To Paxiomadi, Paxi**
MAP B5 ▪ Lakka, Paxi ▪ 26620 33098 ▪ Closed Oct–May ▪ €€
This friendly waterside spot has delicious grilled seafood, meats and traditional sides.

8 **Nionios Taverna, Paxí**
MAP B5 ▪ Lakka, Paxí ▪ 26620 31315 ▪ €
Choose from the fresh daily specials of tasty home-style cooking at this friendly taverna.

9 **Taverna Vasilis, Paxí**
MAP B6 ▪ Main square, Gäios, Paxí ▪ 26620 30062 ▪ €€
Dishes at this traditional taverna include octopus, souvlaki and grills.

10 **Taverna Agni, Corfu**
MAP D2 ▪ Agni Bay, Corfu ▪ 26630 91136 ▪ Closed Oct–May ▪ €€
Freshly caught fish and produce from the owner's garden are used in the dishes at this popular taverna.

Taverna Agni, Corfu

Cafés, Bars and Clubs

① DiZi Bar, Corfu
MAP B3 ■ Ermones, Corfu
■ 698131 4069

DiZi's serves coffees and cocktails by day, and transforms into one of Corfu's liveliest evening venues as the sun goes down.

② Palazzo Cocktail Bar, Corfu
MAP B1 ■ Sidári, Corfu ■ 26630 95946

This lively bar located on Sidári's main thoroughfare serves snacks all day and elaborate cocktails at night.

③ Edem Beach Club
MAP C3 ■ Dasía, Corfu ■ 26610 93013 ■ Closed Sun

A nightlife legend since 1988, Edem is known for its potent cocktails and eclectic dance music. Open from 11am for coffee and snacks, it transforms into a club at sundown.

④ 54 Dreamy Nights, Corfu
MAP D3 ■ Eth. Antistaseos 54, Corfu ■ 69406 45436

Known for its vivid purple lighting and lively club nights – when anything from hip-hop to house and traditional Greek music is played – this luxurious club is a cosmopolitan party venue.

⑤ Harbour Bar, Corfu
MAP D1 ■ The harbour, Kassiópi, Corfu ■ 26630 81227

Relax over morning coffee or evening drinks at this café-bar located at the water's edge at Kassiópi, and enjoy the beautiful views of the sea.

Harbour Bar, Corfu

⑥ 7th Heaven Café, Corfu
Enjoy drinks and grills while taking in a sensational sunset at this west-coast café overlooking Logas beach. It is affiliated to the adjoining Panorama restaurant (see p71).

The beachside bar of La Grótta, Corfu

⑦ La Grótta, Corfu
MAP B3 ■ Paleokastrítsa, Corfu ■ 26630 41006

Be sure to visit this vibrant, subtly lit bar partly housed underground in a cave off the beach. Enjoy the cocktails and light snacks on offer here.

⑧ Four Seasons Café, Paxí
MAP B5 ■ Pórto Longós, Paxí
■ 26620 31829

In a pretty lane not far from the quay, Four Seasons Café is open for breakfast and snacks throughout the day, and then transforms into a cosy restaurant at night.

⑨ Angelos Bar, Corfu
MAP D1 ■ Kassiópi, Corfu
■ 26630 81022

Satellite TVs showing sport and news channels, relaxing seating and music from the 1960s to the 1980s ensure that the Angelos Bar is always lively.

⑩ Mouragio, Paxí
MAP B5 ■ Gaios 490 82, Paxí
■ 69873 33464

This friendly cocktail bar, said to be the first on the island, is directly across from the islet of St Nicholas.

Restaurants

PRICE CATEGORIES

For a three-course meal for one with half a bottle of wine (or equivalent meal), taxes and extra charges.

€ under €30 €€ €30–€50 €€€ over €50

1 The Venetian Well, Corfu
MAP P4 ▪ Lili Desila 1, Corfu Town, Corfu ▪ 26615 50955 ▪ Closed lunch ▪ €€

Dine inside this elegant restaurant, or eat al fresco in its cosy courtyard. À la carte dishes are creatively plated and accompanied by fine wines.

2 Bistro Boileau, Corfu
MAP C3 ▪ Kontokáli, Corfu ▪ 26610 90069 ▪ Closed lunch; Nov–Apr: Sun & Mon ▪ €€€

At this stylish bistro, age-old Greek recipes are given a modern twist, and fine local wines complement the fresh food.

3 Trilogia Restaurant, Corfu
MAP D1 ▪ Seafront Kassiópi, Corfu ▪ 26630 81589 ▪ €€

In a romantic setting overlooking the sea at Kassiópi, Trilogia offers à la carte dishes with a Corfiot twist. The wine list is excellent.

4 Janis Restaurant, Corfu
MAP D1 ▪ Kalamionas Beach, Kassiópi, Corfu ▪ 26630 81082 ▪ €€

With alfresco dining and a superb Greek menu, this popular restaurant serves huge portions of seafood, barbecued meat and Corfiot specialities. Book ahead.

5 Klimataria tou Bellou, Corfu
MAP D4 ▪ Main Square, Benitses, Corfu ▪ 26610 71201 ▪ Closed Apr–Oct: lunch & Sun; Nov–Mar: Mon–Fri ▪ €€

Located in a towering town house that dominates the square, this family-run restaurant serves some of the most imaginative fish dishes in town.

6 La Famiglia, Corfu
MAP P5 ▪ Arlioti Maniarizi 16, Corfu Town, Corfu ▪ 26610 30270 ▪ €€

The elegant La Famiglia celebrates all things Italian with authentic dishes and wines from Italy.

7 Taka Taka, Paxí
MAP B5 ▪ Gäios, Paxí ▪ 26620 32329 ▪ €€

Great barbecued meat and fish dishes are served on a vine-covered terrace. The wine list showcases local vineyards.

8 Akis, Paxí
MAP A5 ▪ Lakka, Paxí ▪ 26620 31247 ▪ Closed Nov–Mar ▪ €

This restaurant is popular for its seafood dishes such as pasta with clams, grilled octopus, and monkfish risotto.

9 Carnagio, Paxí
MAP B5 ▪ Gaios, Paxí ▪ 69741 58814 ▪ €€

The menu here features Paxiot dishes such as *tsilichourdia* (lamb's offal pie) and cuttlefish with fresh vegetables.

Rex restaurant exterior, Corfu Town

10 Rex, Corfu
MAP P5 ▪ Kapodistriou 66, Corfu Town, Corfu ▪ 26610 39649 ▪ €€

Serving Corfiot dishes such as *sofrito* (veal with garlic), this classy restaurant is housed in a fine 19th-century building.

See map on pp62–3

TOP 10 Lefkáda

The smallest prefecture of Greece, Lefkáda comprises one main island and several satellites, including Meganísi, Sparti, Madouri and Skorpidi. The main island, Lefkáda, is connected to the mainland by two bridges that traverse a causeway. At the island's northeastern tip lies its capital, Lefkáda Town, rebuilt after an earthquake in 1948 to the original architectural style. The picturesque island has lush vegetation and a breathtaking, mountainous landscape with olive groves, vineyards and forests of cypress, pine and plane trees. The western coast is rugged, with tiny coves and scenic beaches, such as the beautiful Pórto Katsíki beach, while the east coast has the popular resorts of Nydrí and Perigialia. To the south is Vasilikí Bay, popular with windsurfers.

Enjoying windsurfing near Vasilikí, Lefkáda

LEFKÁDA

Top 10 Sights
see pp74–7

Restaurants
see p81

The Best of the Rest
see p78

Beaches
see p79

Traditional Tavernas
see p80

Flower-filled street in Lefkáda Town

1 Lefkáda Town

The island's characterful capital, Lefkáda Town, was rebuilt after the devastating earthquake of 1948 and comprises unusual buildings of brightly coloured metals and wood, and narrow winding streets that exude charm. Visit the Archaeological Museum, which explores the town's history, and the ruins of the Santa Mávra fortress that dominate the skyline. The fascinating Phonograph Museum, with its collection of old musical instruments, is also worth a visit. Lefkáda's marina is always a hive of activity and offers lively bars, gourmet restaurants and excellent shops (see pp24–5).

2 Lygia

MAP J1 ■ S of Lefkáda Town, Lefkáda

For many, Lygia is just a tiny village that lies along the coastal road from Lefkáda Town to the island's east coast resorts. However, it would be a shame not to stop at this charming place where little has changed over the years. The village's picturesque fishing harbour offers excellent views of the mainland and the mountain village of Néa Plagiá.

3 Nikiana

MAP J2 ■ Below Mount Skaros, east coast, Lefkáda

A small fishing village, Nikiana bustles in the early morning with locals bringing in their catch of freshly caught fish, which is served in its superb tavernas. Water-skiing and windsurfing are popular in the bay, while inland you can explore the traditional villages of Kolyvata and Alexandros.

4 Vlycho

MAP J2 ■ Ormos Vlychos Harbour, Lefkáda

The lively village of Vlycho is especially popular with sailing enthusiasts. The waterfront here is replete with colourful boats of all shapes and sizes bobbing about on the water, or being cleaned or painted. Most tavernas and shops here seem to have adopted a nautical theme.

View over Vlycho bay

⑤ Cavo Nira and Pórto Katsiki

MAP H3 ■ Lipsopirgos peninsula, Lefkáda

Lying on the peninsula that leads to the island's southernmost point, Cape Lefkáda, Cavo Nira and Pórto Katsiki look out over the bay of Vasilikí. According to Greek mythology, the god Apollo was worshipped at a sanctuary near Cavo Nira. The pretty church of St Nikólaos Niras marks the spot. Pórto Katsiki, backed by white cliffs topped with vegetation, is considered to be one of the best beaches in Greece.

LAFCADIO HEARN

As his name suggests, the traveller and scholar Lafcadio Hearn (1850–1904) was born on Lefkáda, the son of a British army officer and a Greek mother. Best known for his writings about Japan, he left the island as an infant and never returned, but is honoured at the Lafcadio Hearn Historical Centre, a joint Japanese-Greek project, which opened in 2014.

⑥ Nydrí

MAP J2 ■ Nydrí waterfalls: NW of Nydrí, east coast, Lefkáda

On the island's east coast lies Nydrí, a pretty town with fabulous views over the islands of Madouri and Sparti, and the tip of Agios Kyriaki on the Greek mainland opposite. A little way out of town, at one end of the Dimosari gorge, are the impressive Nydrí waterfalls. The water here plunges into crystal-clear lakes, which are lovely to swim in during the hot summer months.

Boats anchored off Vasilikí, Lefkáda

⑦ Vasilikí

MAP H2 ■ Ormos Vasilikís cove, Lefkáda

A picturesque village surrounded by forests, Vasilikí is also a busy tourist hotspot as the arrival point for ferries from Kefaloniá and Ithaki. It lies in the Ormos Vasilikís cove, a paradise for sailors and windsurfers due to the strong crosswinds that often blow here. The rich seabed and underwater caves also make Vasilikí a magnet for divers and snorkellers. In addition, the village has white-sand beaches (see p79), and several restaurants and traditional tavernas around the harbour.

⑧ Syvota

MAP J3 ■ Ormos Syvota, Lefkáda

The tiny fishing village of Syvota oozes charm. At the far end of the Ormos Syvota gorge, on Lefkáda's southern coast, it is located about 30 km (19 miles) from the capital. Visitors can enjoy views of the compact bay full of brightly coloured fishing boats and yachts plying their routes across the water, with a backdrop of green rolling hills carpeted with olive

Secluded beach at Syvota

groves. The harbour is lined with ivy-covered tavernas serving fresh seafood. There is a pretty beach here, too.

9 Meganísi
MAP J2

Meganísi, the largest island off Lefkáda, is a green place that retains its rural ideal. According to myth, it was once the island of Krocylea, part of Odysseus's kingdom. Life centres on its capital, the harbour village of Vathý, where ferry boats can be seen plying between here and the mainland. Tavernas specializing in seafood line Vathý harbour and are busy with day-trippers. Along the coast are the small harbours of Atheni and Spartochori, while inland is the unspoiled village of Katomeri. Off-shore, and part of Meganísi municipality, lie the islands of Sparti and Skorpios.

Waterfall in Dimosari Gorge

10 Dimosari Gorge
MAP J2 ■ E of Nydrí, Lefkáda

With rugged rock faces, lakes, ponds, waterfalls and forests, the stunning Dimosari gorge slices through the east coast near Perigialia and Nydrí and heads inland towards the mountain villages of Vafkeri and Englouvi. Nature trails can be followed around parts of the gorge, and the rock face can be scaled by climbing enthusiasts.

A MORNING ON THE EAST COAST

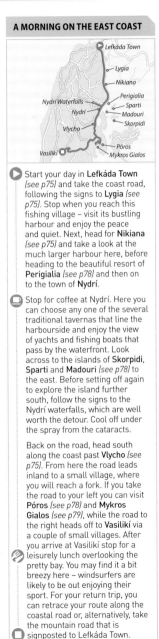

Start your day in **Lefkáda Town** (see p75) and take the coast road, following the signs to **Lygia** (see p75). Stop when you reach this fishing village – visit its bustling harbour and enjoy the peace and quiet. Next, head for **Nikiana** (see p75) and take a look at the much larger harbour here, before heading to the beautiful resort of **Perigialia** (see p78) and then on to the town of **Nydrí**.

Stop for coffee at Nydrí. Here you can choose any one of the several traditional tavernas that line the harbourside and enjoy the view of yachts and fishing boats that pass by the waterfront. Look across to the islands of **Skorpidi**, **Sparti** and **Madouri** (see p78) to the east. Before setting off again to explore the island further south, follow the signs to the Nydrí waterfalls, which are well worth the detour. Cool off under the spray from the cataracts.

Back on the road, head south along the coast past **Vlycho** (see p75). From here the road leads inland to a small village, where you will reach a fork. If you take the road to your left you can visit **Póros** (see p78) and **Mykros Gialos** (see p79), while the road to the right heads off to **Vasilikí** via a couple of small villages. After you arrive at Vasilikí stop for a leisurely lunch overlooking the pretty bay. You may find it a bit breezy here – windsurfers are likely to be out enjoying their sport. For your return trip, you can retrace your route along the coastal road or, alternatively, take the mountain road that is signposted to Lefkáda Town.

See map on p74

The Best of the Rest

 1 Kalamítsi
MAP H2

With its panoramic views over a crescent-shaped bay, Kalamítsi, which is built on a hillside, is one of the most beautiful spots on Lefkáda. Also one of the oldest villages on the island, it is known for its windmills and churches.

2 Sparti Island
MAP J2 ■ NE of Nydrí, east coast, Lefkáda

Sparti is the most northerly of the huddle of islands that lie off the east coast of Lefkáda. It is characterized by dense green undergrowth that extends to its coastline.

3 Skorpidi Island
MAP J2 ■ W of Nydrí, Lefkáda

This is one of the smallest islands off Lefkadá. Its unspoiled countryside and coastline offer great opportunities for exploration. You can take a boat across from Nydrí for a relaxing day trip.

4 Perigialia
MAP J2 ■ Near Nydrí, Lefkáda

Best known for its 15th-century church where, in the 19th century, revolutionaries hid out against the British Protectorate, Perigialia is now a popular spot for visitors keen to experience a taste of village life.

5 Madouri Island
MAP J2 ■ NW of Nydrí, Lefkáda

This small island, covered in greenery, is tucked into the bay off Nydrí, between the town and the island of Sparti. It is easily accessed by boat.

View of Madouri Island

 6 Póros
MAP J2 ■ Ormos Rouda, Lefkáda

With its tiny alleyways and pretty bougainvillea-covered stone houses, Póros is a must-see. The Church of Analipsi here has some notable 16th-century icons, and there are the ruins of a fortress nearby.

7 Sivros
MAP H2 ■ N of Vasilikí, Lefkáda

Lying in the heart of Lefkadá is the remote mountain village of Sivros, which comprises a cluster of stone houses surrounded by laurel woods. It has very few modern amenities.

 8 Kariá
MAP H2

Often known as Karyá, this pretty mountain village is situated in central Lefkadá and has managed to retain its traditional way of life. The popular local craft of intricate embroidery continues to flourish here.

9 Cape Lefkáda
MAP H3

Although exposed and barren, this peninsula, the island's southernmost point, is nonetheless enchanting, with its sheer cliffs that contrast sharply with the blue of the sea. It is reached by a tiny, uneven road.

10 Agios Nikitas
MAP H1 ■ SW of Lefkáda Town, Lefkáda

A short drive from Lefkáda Town takes you to this small fishing village, which has been transformed into one of the island's prettiest and smartest resorts.

Beaches

Overlooking Mýlos Beach, Lefkáda

1 Mýlos Beach
This scenic beach is famous for its iconic 18th-century stone windmill, which would not look out of place on a postcard. Today, the old building functions as a café. Steps lead down to the soft sandy beach *(see p25)*.

2 Egremini Beach
MAP H2 ■ Athani, Lefkáda
Not to be confused with a smaller beach of the same name found near Agios Nikitas, the stunning Egremini beach lies close to Athani village. It can be accessed only by a tiny road.

3 Mykros Gialos Beach
MAP J2 ■ Ormos Rouda, Lefkáda
Lying in the Ormos Rouda bay, just south of Póros, is the pebble beach of Mykros Gialos. It is a popular summer holiday destination.

4 Megalo Limonari Beach
MAP J2 ■ Near Katomerí, Meganísi
Remote and very beautiful, Megalo Limonari beach (on the island of Meganísi) can be accessed from Katomerí village on Meganísi's south coast. It is sandy, surrounded by trees and sits in an attractive bay.

5 Pefkoulia Beach
MAP H1 ■ N of Agios Nikitas, Lefkáda
This popular beach is a large sweep of sand on the west coast near Agios Nikitas. The turquoise water offers ideal swimming conditions.

6 Nikiana Beach
MAP J2 ■ Nikiana, Lefkáda
Not far from the village of Nikiana, this beach is one of the sandiest in the area. There are tavernas and bars here to serve holidaymakers.

7 Vasilikí Beach
MAP H2 ■ Ormos Vasilikís, Lefkáda
Vasilikí beach is best known for its excellent sailing and windsurfing conditions. Dedicated clubs provide both instruction and equipment.

8 Kathísma Beach
MAP H2 ■ Kalamítsi, Lefkáda
One of the most visited beaches on Lefkáda, Kathísma beach is long and wide, and boasts soft white sand.

Parasols along Kathísma Beach

9 Póros Beach
MAP J2 ■ Ormos Rouda, Lefkáda
Póros beach lies south of the town of the same name. It is quieter than its neighbour, Mykros Gialos, and is favoured by visitors who like camping.

10 Gialos Beach
MAP H2 ■ Athani, Lefkáda
This shingle beach can be reached via a steep, winding road followed by a series of tracks. Its tranquil feel makes the journey worthwhile.

See map on p74

Traditional Tavernas

Fryni Sto Mólos
MAP J1 ■ Golemi, Lefkáda Town, Lefkáda ■ 26450 24879 ■ €

Delicious souvlaki and dips are served here in an endless stream of mezes, accompanied by local wine and beer.

2 Zolithros
MAP J2 ■ Mykros Gialos, Lefkáda ■ 69723 18385 ■ Closed Oct–May ■ €

This quintessential taverna serves fish straight from the owner's boat, as well as traditional meat dishes.

3 Taverna Pantazis
MAP J2 ■ Nikiana, Lefkáda ■ 26450 71211 ■ €€

Popular with locals, Pantazis offers a wide choice of fish and seafood. House specials are lobster and lamb.

4 O Molos
MAP J2 ■ Harbour, Mykros Gialos, Lefkáda ■ 26450 95548 ■ Closed lunch ■ €

The homemade dishes at this taverna include local specialities such as fresh seafood platters and *moussaka*.

5 Café Liotrivi
MAP J3 ■ Syvota, Lefkáda ■ 26450 31870 ■ Closed Nov–Apr ■ €

Overlooking the bay, this atmospheric café/taverna is housed in a former olive-oil press. It offers breakfast and light Greek food.

PRICE CATEGORIES

For a three-course meal for one with half a bottle of wine (or equivalent meal), taxes and extra charges.

€ under €30 ■ €€ €30–€50 ■ €€€ over €50

6 Taverna Kanioria
MAP J1 ■ Lygia, Lefkáda ■ 26450 72229 ■ Closed lunch ■ €

Enjoy classic Greek dishes, such as *afelia* (marinated pork), and excellent views of the harbour at this friendly, family-run taverna.

7 Keramidaki Taverna
MAP J2 ■ Nikiana, Lefkáda ■ 26450 92417 ■ €€

Mature olive trees offer shade on the charming terrace here, and the menu features superb herb-infused seafood.

8 Taverna Oasis
MAP H3 ■ Pórto Katsiki, Lefkáda ■ 26450 33201 ■ €

Shaded by trees and offering great sea views, Taverna Oasis is popular with locals and serves goat, rabbit and other meats straight off the coals.

9 Taverna Lakis
MAP J2 ■ Spartochóri, Meganísi island ■ 26450 51228 ■ Closed lunch ■ €€

Homemade local food is served at this bougainvillea-covered taverna located on a typical picturesque cobbled alleyway in Spartochóri village on Meganísi island.

10 Seven Islands
MAP J1 ■ Lygia, Lefkáda ■ 26450 71747 ■ Closed Nov–Apr ■ €€

This seaside taverna offers a good variety of vegetarian dishes, as well as seafood, grills and pastries.

Café Liotrivi, seen from Syvota Bay

Restaurants

 Basilico
MAP J2 ■ Harbour, Nydrí, Lefkáda ■ 26450 93121 ■ €€

Run by a local family, this popular restaurant serves classic Greek meat, fish and vegetarian dishes and heavenly homemade desserts.

 Rachi
MAP H2 ■ Exanthia, Lefkáda ■ 26450 99439 ■ Closed Nov–Apr ■ €€

Famous for the sunset views from its dining verandah, Rachi serves classic dishes such as moussaka and souvlaki. It also has an inspired cocktail menu.

3 **Tropicana Restaurant**
MAP J2 ■ Spartochóri, Meganísi island ■ 26450 51486 ■ €

Located in the centre of Spartochóri village and with views out towards Lefkáda, Tropicana Restaurant is known for its homemade pizzas and chargrilled souvlaki.

4 **Giannis**
MAP J1 ■ Lygia, Lefkáda ■ 26450 71619 ■ €

This family-run restaurant has a traditionally Greek menu. There are plenty of choices to please those with a sweet tooth, such as homemade *bourko* and *kadaifi*, as well as fruit and nut jams.

5 **Kyma**
MAP J1 ■ Plataeia Foinikis, Lefkada Town ■ 26450 22280 ■ €€

Popular with locals for its *kakavia* (fish soup), fresh catch of the day and delicious traditional desserts, this restaurant is a great place to try local food with views of the sea.

6 **The Barrel**
MAP J2 ■ Nydrí Marina, Nydrí, Lefkada ■ 26450 92906 ■ €€

A good mix of international dishes and Greek cuisine, as well as a wide variety of wines, is served at this open-air restaurant at the marina.

7 **Duende**
MAP J2 ■ Nikiana, Lefkáda ■ 26450 72383 ■ €

Enjoy elegantly presented and creative upscale Mediterranean and Greek cuisine as well as the delicious recipes of the Ionian at this lovely resort restaurant.

View from Porto Nikiana restaurant

8 **Porto Nikiana**
MAP J2 ■ Nikiana, Lefkáda ■ 26450 71746 ■ €€

The combination of excellent barbecued meat and fish, imaginative salads and desserts, plus a location right beside the sea at Nikiana harbour, has put this friendly taverna on the map.

9 **Thymari**
MAP J1 ■ Pinelopis 19, Lefkáda Town ■ 26450 22266 ■ Closed lunch ■ €

The emphasis at Thymari is on traditional Greek dishes with a modern Mediterranean twist. The wine list is strong on local wines.

10 **Minas**
MAP J2 ■ Nikiana, Lefkáda ■ 26450 71480 ■ €€€

This pretty restaurant overlooking the bay serves fresh fish caught by its own fishing crew and seasoned with herbs from its garden.

See map on p74 »

TOP 10 Kefaloniá and Ithaki

Beautiful, rugged and densely forested, Kefaloniá is the largest island in the Ionians and the sixth-largest in Greece. It is dominated

Roman Villa floor mosaic, Kefaloniá

by Mount Eros (Aínos) which, at 1,600 m (5,200 ft), is the highest peak in the archipelago. Dramatic scenery can be found everywhere. Subterranean waterways, caves, pebbly beaches, wild mountain slopes and natural springs all feature. The island of Ithaki lies off the northeast coast – an unspoiled idyll widely believed to have been the home of King Odysseus. Like Kefaloniá, Ithaki is thought to have been inhabited since prehistoric times.

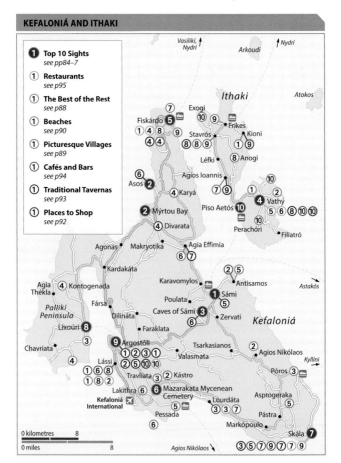

KEFALONIÁ AND ITHAKI

1 Top 10 Sights
see pp84–7

1 Restaurants
see p95

1 The Best of the Rest
see p88

1 Beaches
see p90

1 Picturesque Villages
see p89

1 Cafés and Bars
see p94

1 Traditional Tavernas
see p93

1 Places to Shop
see p92

Previous pages Boats bobbing in the clear waters off Navagio Bay, Zákynthos

Antísamos Beach near the port of Sámi, Kefaloniá

1 Sámi, Kefaloniá
MAP H5 ■ East coast, Kefaloniá

Sámi lies northeast of the capital, Argostóli, on the island's east coast and is Kefaloniá main port. This attractive town has traditional-style buildings overlooking the bay, which bustles with boats and ferries. It has a good choice of restaurants and bars, and popular sights include the pebbly beach of Antísamos (see p90), nearby Karavomylos and many local caves.

2 Asos and Mýrtou Bay, Kefaloniá

An unspoiled village that lies just north of Mýrtou Bay, Asos can be reached by a sharply descending road from a stone terrace to the sea. It sits in a small harbour and boasts charming traditional architecture. A small isthmus reaches out from its harbourside to the remains of a Venetian castle that protected the village in ancient times. Minutes away is the stunning Mýrtou Bay with its famous turquoise sea, horseshoe-shaped white beach and cliff backdrop. It is widely considered to be one of the most beautiful bays in the world (see pp28–9).

3 Caves of Sámi, Kefaloniá

Drogaráti cave is a wonder of nature. Believed to be over a million years old, this huge space was discovered more than 300 years ago when an earthquake revealed its entrance. Incredible stalactites and stalagmites can be seen by visitors on their way to the Royal Balcony, a natural rock platform, and the Chamber of Exaltation, now an operatic concert venue. Other caves include Angalaki, the largest in the area, and Melissáni, where artifacts dating from the 4th century BC have been discovered (see pp30–31).

Lake in Melissáni cave, Kefaloniá

4 Vathý, Ithaki
MAP J4

The capital and port of Ithaki, Vathý is believed to have been built on the ancient Homeric harbour of Phorkys. Records suggest it was an important trading port in medieval times. In the 17th century, the town's architecture was strongly influenced by the Heptanesian art movement of the day. Although severely damaged in the 1953 earthquake, Vathý was rebuilt, and its whitewashed houses hint at its former glory. Some original houses can still be seen.

The pretty waterside village of Fiskárdo, Kefaloniá

5 Fiskárdo, Kefaloniá
MAP H4 ■ North coast, Kefaloniá

The only village in Kefaloniá to have escaped damage in the 1953 earthquake, Fiskárdo is home to original pastel-coloured Venetian buildings, and a busy marina and ferry dock. Seafood restaurants, tavernas and bars ensure its popularity. Surrounded by a landscape clothed in cypress trees, it offers wonderful views of neighbouring island Ithaki.

6 Mazarakata Mycenean Cemetery
MAP H6 ■ 9 km (6 miles) SE of Argostóli, Kefaloniá

Discovered in 1908, this ancient cemetery is considered to be the largest Mycenean graveyard found on the island to date. It has revealed 17 subterranean chamber tombs carved into the natural rock. They were found intact, filled with colourful amphorae, glass vessels and other burial offerings.

EARTHQUAKES IN THE IONIANS

The Ionians lie on a major geological fault, where the European and Aegean tectonic plates meet. Tension between the plates creates ongoing seismic activity; this is usually minor, but a few times each century, earthquakes occur. The largest in recent years, at 7.2 on the Richter scale, was on 12 August 1953. Its epicentre lay just off Kefaloniá.

7 Skála, Kefaloniá
MAP J6 ■ Southeast coast, Kefaloniá

An attractive town on the southeastern tip of the island, Skála offers a good choice of sandy beaches, restaurants, hotels, attractions for children, shops and nightlife. The earthquake of 1953 destroyed much of the town's original architecture, the remains of which can still be seen. A short distance from the town are beautiful pine forests, and further inland you will find the Roman Villa, an archaeological site with some well-preserved mosaics that once adorned the floor of an impressive mansion.

8 Lixoúri, Kefaloniá
MAP G5 ■ Pallikí peninsula, Kefaloniá

An elegant town that can trace its history back to before Venetian times, Lixoúri has steadily flourished over the years. In the 19th and 20th centuries, it was a holiday destination favoured by writers, poets and the Greek royal family. Today, after many of its buildings were rebuilt following the 1953 earthquake, Lixoúri is the island's second largest community after Argostóli. It sits on the Pallikí Peninsula opposite the capital.

9 Argostóli, Kefaloniá

A charming town lying in a large bay, Argostóli is the capital of Kefaloniá (see pp26–7). Life here revolves around the central square,

A DAY TRIP FROM ARGOSTÓLI TO FISKÁRDO

▶ MORNING

For a great day out from the capital of Kefaloniá, **Argostóli**, take the coast road to Fiskárdo village, located at the island's northern tip. After a hearty breakfast at one of Argostóli's tavernas, head north until you begin to see signs for **Mýrtou Bay** *(see p85)* around Agonas. The view of the coastline is breathtaking. Head for the steeply descending road that winds down to the stunning Mýrtou Bay and stop for a break at the bottom. There is a small taverna here, although little else. Refresh yourself, take some photographs and enjoy what is considered to be one of the most beautiful beaches in the world. For great views of the bay from above, go to one of the special viewing areas along the road.

AFTERNOON

After taking pictures of the bay, head back up the road and follow the signposts towards the village of **Asos** *(see p85)*. Lying in an attractive harbour, this village is an ideal place to stop for lunch. There are a handful of good tavernas here that look out over the water. After refreshments, carry on to **Fiskárdo**. The road will take you a little inland here, through some small and very picturesque hamlets. This part of the journey should take only about 30 minutes; more if you stop to admire the scenery. Fiskárdo is a great place to explore before making your way back to Argostóli by retracing your route, or taking the east coast road via **Sámi** *(see p85)*.

Plateia Valliánou. A hive of activity, it is lined with great restaurants, while the Lithóstrot, the main shopping street, has superb shops. Argostóli was almost entirely destroyed in the 1953 earthquake, but has since been rebuilt in keeping with its former architectural style. The Historical and Folk Museum has a collection of photographs showing the destruction and rebuilding of the town.

Shopping street in Argostóli

⑩ Piso Aetós, Ithaki
MAP J4 ■ **W of Vathý, Ithaki**

Sleepy Piso Aetós lies on an isthmus of land linking north and south Ithaki, and is the arrival point for boats from Kefaloniá. In ancient times, it was the location of the ancient acropolis of Alalkomenes, believed by some to be the site of Odysseus's palace. The beach here is pebbly but pretty.

See map on p84 ←

The Best of the Rest

 1 Lazareto Island, Ithaki
MAP J4 ■ Off Vathý, Ithaki

Once used as a *lazaretto*, or quarantine station, this island has a collection of Venetian buildings and a chapel. It is a memorable sight as you pass by on a boat into the harbour at Vathý.

2 Lake Avythos, Kefaloniá
MAP J5 ■ Near Agios Nikólaos, Kefaloniá

Surrounded by trees and with Mount Eros in the distance, the large inland lake of Avythos is an enchanting sight.

3 Póros, Kefaloniá
MAP J6 ■ Southeast coast, Kefaloniá

This quiet fishing town has a long beach, a small marina and a few good tavernas. Nearby is the Monastery of Sissia, the oldest on the island.

4 Kontogenada, Kefaloniá
MAP G5 ■ Pallikí peninsula, Kefaloniá

Lying in the centre of the Pallikí peninsula, this small village is famous as the site of some Mycenaean tombs. It also has a couple of churches with some notable post-Byzantine icons.

 5 Pessada, Kefaloniá
MAP H6 ■ South coast, Kefaloniá

A beautiful, unspoiled bay with soft sand and clear waters not far from Argostóli, Pessada is where the capital's residents go to relax. Access is via a small path from the road.

 6 Dia Island, Kefaloniá
MAP H6 ■ Off Argostóli, Kefaloniá

Sometimes known as Theionisi, Dia Island is the source of many legends. The most popular of these claims that it was home to a temple dedicated to the Greek god Zeus.

7 Lourdáta, Kefaloniá
MAP H6 ■ Ormos Lourdáta, Kefaloniá

Lying on the island's south coast, the picture-postcard fishing harbour and village of Lourdáta boasts a glorious sand and pebble beach. Nearby is a 13th-century monastery.

8 Bay of Polis, Ithaki
MAP H4 ■ Off Stavrós, Ithaki

This is the location of the Loizos cave, where Athena, Artemis and Hera, the Greek goddesses, were believed to have been worshipped in ancient times.

9 Frikes, Ithaki
MAP H4 ■ N of Vathý, Ithaki

This tiny village is ideal for visitors who want to experience local life. It has a pretty harbour from where ferries regularly ply to Lefkáda and Kefaloniá.

10 Perachóri, Ithaki
MAP J4 ■ Near Vathý, Ithaki

A monastery dedicated to the Taxiarchs – the Archangels Michael and Gabriel – dominates this small village, which is also known for its fine locally produced organic food.

Picturesque Pessada bay

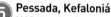

Picturesque Villages

The port village of Kioni on Ithaki

1 Kioni, Ithaki
MAP J4 ■ Near Frikes, Ithaki

One of the few villages that was untouched by the 1953 earthquake, upmarket Kioni has lovely centuries-old buildings, including windmills.

2 Kastro, Kefaloniá
MAP H6 ■ Near Pessada, Kefaloniá

This delightful village is characterized by whitewashed Venetian houses and dominated by the Byzantine fortress of Agios Georgios. An unassuming place, it was once the capital of the island.

3 Travliata, Kefaloniá
MAP H6 ■ NW of Lourdáta, Kefaloniá

Life in Travliata revolves around local farming. Views over the surrounding countryside are fabulous. Most of the buildings here were rebuilt after the devastating earthquake of 1953.

4 Karyá, Kefaloniá
MAP H4

Karyá is one of several mountain villages, including Vary, Patrikáta and Konitáta, where life appears to have remained unchanged for centuries. The views from this high vantage point are breathtaking.

5 Asprogeraka, Kefaloniá
MAP J6 ■ Inland from Póros, Kefaloniá

A quiet village surrounded by olive groves, Asprogeraka is famous for being the site of some important Mycenaean wall ruins.

6 Lakithra, Kefaloniá
MAP H6 ■ Near Argostóli, Kefaloniá

Despite its location near the airport, Lakithra manages to retain its traditional feel. Take in the coastal panoramas at almost every turn.

7 Agios Ioannis, Ithaki
MAP H4

This village is one of the prettiest and most atmospheric on the island. Its bougainvillea-draped houses, tiny streets and sea views are captivating.

8 Anogi, Ithaki
MAP J4 ■ Near Kioni, Ithaki

This place is known for its pretty stone houses and the attractive Church of the Dormition of the Virgin, adorned with Byzantine frescoes. Located on Mount Niritos, it has great sea views.

Interior of Anogi church, Ithaki

9 Stavrós, Ithaki
MAP H4 ■ Bay of Polis, Ithaki

The village of Stavrós is Ithaki's second-largest community. Its numerous Venetian houses managed to survive the 1953 earthquake and lend the village historic charm.

10 Exogi, Ithaki
MAP H4 ■ Near Stavrós, Ithaki

Ithaki's northernmost village, Exogi is a remote place where the only sound that can be heard is birdsong. High above the coast, it has great views over the water towards Kefaloniá.

See map on p84

Beaches

1 Makrýs Gialos Beach, Kefaloniá

MAP G6 ■ Lássi, Kefaloniá

Sometimes spelled Makrýs Yalos, this beach has lovely fine sand and clear and safe water in which to swim. It lies a little way south of Argostóli.

Sarakiniko beach, Ithaki

2 Sarakiniko Beach, Ithaki

MAP J4 ■ Vathý, Ithaki

Popular with swimmers because of its safe waters, Sarakiniko lies just west of Vathý. Sit, relax and watch as boats are manoeuvred in and out of the lively anchorage.

3 Lepeda Beach, Kefaloniá

MAP G5 ■ Pallikí peninsula, Kefaloniá

Unusual rock formations are a striking sight off Lepeda beach, a quiet stretch of red sand along the coast south of Lixoúri. The views across the bay to Argostóli are breathtaking.

4 Xi Beach, Kefaloniá

MAP G6 ■ Pallikí peninsula, Kefaloniá

One of the most popular of the Pallikí peninsula's south-coast beaches, Xi has deep red sands and safe swimming waters. It is located just a short distance from Lixoúri.

5 Antísamos Beach, Kefaloniá

MAP J5 ■ Sámi, Kefaloniá

This outstanding beach is one of Sámi's best swimming spots. It appeared in the 2001 film, *Captain Corelli's Mandolin* (see p29).

6 Agia Effimia Beach, Kefaloniá

MAP H5 ■ Sámi, Kefaloniá

This fishing village is popular with sailors who moor in its harbour. The beach here, which runs along the east coast, is long but pebbly.

7 Emplysi Beach, Kefaloniá

MAP H3 ■ Fiskárdo, Kefaloniá

One of Fiskárdo's premier beaches, Emplysi emerges at the end of a small track surrounded by olive groves and cypress trees. It lies in a sheltered bay a little more than 1 km (half a mile) from the village.

8 Platýs Gialos Beach, Kefaloniá

MAP G6 ■ Lássi, Kefaloniá

Further along the coast from Makrýs Gialos is Platýs Gialos beach, linked to a small island by an isthmus. It has fine, soft sand and is popular with watersports enthusiasts.

9 Foki Beach, Kefaloniá

MAP H4 ■ Fiskárdo, Kefaloniá

Less a beach and more a rocky outcrop, Foki, with its shady trees and clear blue water, remains one of the most popular spots around Fiskárdo.

10 Gidaki Beach, Ithaki

MAP J4 ■ Near Vathý, Ithaki

Offering the chance to relax away from the crowds, this beach is accessed only by a hiking track. However, boats do arrive from Vathý every day during summer.

Turquoise waters lapping an Ithaki beach

Outdoor Activities

Pleasure boats off the pretty harbourside village of Asos, Kefaloniá

1 Sailing
Large yachts and motor cruisers can be hired here, provided you possess the right qualifications. Smaller boats are also available at most of the holiday hotspots and are ideal for exploring the little coves dotted around the islands.

2 Nature Trails
Other than the Mount Eros National Park in southern Kefaloniá, the two islands have only a handful of designated nature trails. However, excellent maps are available to help you chart your own trail.

3 Swimming

Both islands are blessed with beautifully clear water, and swimming is a popular activity. However, there are strong currents along the west coast, at places such as Mýrtou Bay, where caution should be exercised.

4 Diving and Snorkelling

The indented coastlines of Kefaloniá and Ithaki, with their caves and rocks, are a dream for snorkellers and divers. The region's clear water means that there is excellent visibility.

5 Archaeological Tours
Hotels often have details of organized archaeological tours to nearby sites. Other places, such as the mosaics at Skála's Roman Villa or the Palaiochóra ruins *(see p41)*, can be explored privately.

6 Cycling
Mountain bikes can be hired on both Kefaloniá and Ithaki, although the nature of the terrain can make cycling a challenging pursuit. However, ordinary bicycles are also available at most hotels and resorts, and from private companies.

7 Sea Kayaking
This sport is becoming increasingly popular around Kefaloniá's sheltered coves, secluded beaches and sea caves. It is easy for any reasonably fit visitor.

8 Horse Riding
Taking an organized ride into the lush countryside can be a wonderful way to see both islands. There are a few stables and small riding schools that offer this outdoor activity.

9 Watersports

Beaches such as Makrýs Gialos at Lássi and Lepeda and Xi at Lixoúri *(see p90)*, offer some great watersports opportunities. Windsurfing and water-skiing are two of the most popular of these activities.

10 Walking

Both Kefaloniá and Ithaki are ideal destinations for people who enjoy walking. Ithaki, especially, has several designated hiking paths that take in the island's villages and best views. Details are available from Ithaki's tourist office.

See map on p84

Places to Shop

① Tzannatos, Kefaloniá
MAP G5 ■ Lithostratho 40, Argostóli, Kefalonia ■ 26710 28665

This family-run shop has been selling beautiful jewellery made by hand in gold, silver and other precious metals since 1904.

② Garbis, Kefaloniá
MAP G5 ■ 24 Lithostroto, Argostóli ■ 26710 23164

Owned by Nick Garbis, who designed the period jewellery worn by Penelope Cruz in the film *Captain Corelli's Mandolin*, this shop sells handmade contemporary pieces and replicas of ancient jewellery in gold, silver and precious stones.

Garbis jeweller, Kefaloniá

③ Down the Rabbit Hole
MAP G5 ■ Livostrathou, Argostóli, Kefaloniá
■ 26714 00274

After settling here from Yorkshire, Karen Fozzard set up this tiny boutique – a treasuretrove of original but affordable paintings, crafts, enamelware and other types of jewellery.

④ Myrtillo
MAP H4 ■ Divarata, Kefaloniá
■ 26747 70145

A great shop for gifts, Myrtillo sells speciality food and wine from the island, including local herbs and spices, honey, olives and sweets.

⑤ IN Gallery
MAP H5 ■ Agglias 16, Sámi, Kefaloniá ■ 26740 22885

Dramatic paintings of the island, religious icons, ceramics and handcrafted jewellery are among the gifts available at this trendy gallery in Sámi.

⑥ Annikas Greek Handicrafts
MAP H5 ■ Drogaráti Cave, Sámi, Kefaloniá ■ 69387 62384

Watch demonstrations of wood-turning and other handicrafts at this workshop and shop at the entrance to Drogaráti Cave. Unusual souvenirs abound.

⑦ Mandola
MAP J6 ■ Skála, Kefaloniá
■ 26701 83176 ■ Closed Oct–May

With its cottage-chic decor and crafted items along a similar theme, this shop is both pleasing on the eye and a great place in which to find a souvenir.

⑧ Alikis Store
MAP H4 ■ Stavros, Ithaki
■ 26740 32110 ■ Closed Oct–May

This fantastic little shop sells all things Ithakian and Greek, such as handmade crafts, liqueurs, preserves, organic honey, jams, herbs and confectionery.

⑨ Amfitriti Jewellery
MAP J4 ■ Kioni, Ithaki
■ 26740 31034 ■ Closed Oct–May

Handmade gold and silver necklaces, pendants and bracelets are sold here, along with paintings, ceramics, olive wood souvenirs, woven rugs and other gifts.

⑩ Nostalgia, Ithaki
MAP J4 ■ Vathý, Ithaki
■ 26740 33113

Featuring collections from several artisans, this lovely shop offers an interesting selection of jewellery, housewares and gifts.

Traditional Tavernas

PRICE CATEGORIES

For a three-course meal for one with half a bottle of wine (or equivalent meal), taxes and extra charges.

€ under €30 €€ €30–€50 €€€ over €50

1 Patsouras
MAP G5 ▪ Leof. Antoni Tritsi, Argostóli, Kefaloniá ▪ 26711 02960 ▪ €€

The local dish *krasáto* – pork cooked in wine and herbs – is a speciality of this taverna. Be sure to dine outside on the pretty terrace.

2 Palia Plaka
MAP G5 ▪ Ioannis Metaxa 2, Argostóli, Kefaloniá ▪ 26710 24849 ▪ €

The menu features typical island dishes such as seafood pie, rabbit stew and scrambled eggs with tomato. Locals say this taverna has the best traditional food on Kefaloniá.

3 Apostolis Taverna
MAP J6 ▪ Skála, Kefaloniá ▪ 26710 83013 ▪ Closed Oct–May ▪ €€

Dine inside or al fresco on the terrace at this popular taverna known for its wholesome country dishes such as veal *stifado* (stew) and lamb souvlaki.

4 Nicolas Taverna
MAP H4 ▪ Fiskárdo, Kefaloniá ▪ 26740 41307 ▪ €€

On a balcony overlooking the charming harbor of Fiskárdo, this lovely taverna offers classic Greek dishes and local specialities of Kefaloniá.

5 Ladokolla
MAP J3 ▪ Davi 13, Argostóli, Kefaloniá ▪ 26710 25522 ▪ €

Huge dishes such as pork *krasáto* (braised in wine), souvlaki and grilled chicken with accompaniments are served quirkily on paper. Diners who like a particularly informal setting will have fun here.

6 Platanos
MAP H4 ▪ Asos, Kefaloniá ▪ 26740 51381 ▪ €€

A vast plane tree provides shade to diners enjoying fresh dishes cooked to perfection at this lovely seafood restaurant.

Platanos taverna in Asos, Kefaloniá

7 Perasma Grill
MAP H5 ▪ Agia Efimia, Kefaloniá ▪ 26740 61990 ▪ €€

This taverna is known for its organic produce and a menu based on recipes handed down through generations.

8 Trehantiri
MAP J4 ▪ Vathý, Ithaki ▪ 26740 33444 ▪ Closed Oct–May ▪ €€

Traditional homemade local dishes using fresh ingredients draw crowds to this long-standing family taverna.

9 Chani
Odos Kioniou, Pera Pigadiou, Agios Ioannis, Ithaki ▪ 68424 87436 ▪ €

This roadside taverna specilizies in goat meat dishes and has fabulous views across the strait.

10 El Greco Taverna
MAP G5 ▪ Vasil Vandoru 1, Argostóli, Kefaloniá ▪ 26710 24449 ▪ €€

Popular with locals, El Greco offers a taste of rural Kefaloniá in the heart of town. Its menu offers authentic home cooking.

See map on p84

Cafés and Bars

① Nefeli
MAP G6 ▪ Lássi, Kefaloniá
▪ 26710 25203

A family-run taverna, Nefeli serves traditional Mediterranean breakfasts, snacks and light meals cooked in its wood-fired oven.

② Antisomatos Beach Bar
MAP H5 ▪ Antisamos Beach, Sámi, Kefaloniá ▪ 69446 76863
▪ Closed Oct–May

Surrounded by palm trees, this laid-back beach bar serves cocktails, cold beers and juices all day, plus bistro-style burgers and seafood.

③ Café Bar Muses
MAP H6 ▪ Lourdáta, Kefaloniá
▪ 26710 31175

Big screens showing the day's sports events, good music and a menu of cocktails, coffees and snacks ensure this bar is always lively.

④ Le Passage
MAP H4 ▪ Harbour, Fiskárdo, Kefaloniá ▪ 26740 41505
▪ Closed Oct–May

This super-trendy café, decorated in a modern cottage-chic style, tempts visitors with a menu of cocktails, fruit shakes, coffees and delicious snacks.

⑤ Veto Bar
MAP J6 ▪ Skála, Kefaloniá
▪ 26710 83015

The large, bright Veto Bar is known for its colourful cocktails. It also offers light snacks and beers, as well as television screens showing sports events.

⑥ Logos Grand View Cocktail Bar
MAP G6 ▪ Lássi, Kefaloniá ▪ 26714 00005 ▪ Closed Oct–May

The hillside terrace of this lively lounge-bar offers stunning coastal sunset views. The bar serves reasonably priced cocktails and bistro food.

⑦ Captain's Lounge Bar
MAP J6 ▪ Skála, Kefaloniá
▪ 26710 83389 ▪ Closed Oct–May

Almost any cocktail imaginable is on the menu at this elegant, popular bar with an open-air terrace and welcoming hosts.

⑧ Eden Bar
MAP G6 ▪ Lássi, Kefaloniá
▪ 26710 26734 ▪ Closed Oct–May

Set in exotic gardens, this bar has great cocktails and a convivial atmosphere, which have earned it a great reputation.

⑨ Akri Seaside Bar
MAP J6 ▪ Skála, Kefaloniá
▪ 26710 83229

Enjoy some of the most creative cocktails in Skála at this bar, which also has music and dancing.

⑩ Karamela Café
MAP J4 ▪ Harbour, Vathý, Ithaki
▪ 26740 33567 ▪ Closed Oct–May

This lovely café offers honey-drenched pastries, cakes and coffee, as well as cocktails and live music.

Veto Bar, Kefaloniá

Restaurants

1 Tassia
MAP H4 ▪ Fiskárdo Harbour, Kefaloniá ▪ 26740 41265 ▪ Closed Nov–Apr ▪ €€€

Run by Tassia Dendrinou, an acclaimed chef and author, this restaurant is famed for its fine seafood dishes and wine list.

2 Blue Sky Restaurant
MAP G6 ▪ Lássi, Kefaloniá ▪ 26710 22713 ▪ Closed Nov–Apr ▪ €€

One of Lássi's trendiest places to eat, the spacious Blue Sky Restaurant offers creative Greek dishes. There is also live music some evenings.

3 Andromeda Restaurant
MAP H6 ▪ Lourdas, Livathos, Kefaloniá ▪ 26710 31413 ▪ Closed Nov–Apr ▪ €€

Set in its own gardens overlooking the bay, the Andromeda specializes in upmarket Greek cuisine, with each dish artfully presented.

4 Elli's
MAP H4 ▪ Harbour, Fiskárdo, Kefaloniá ▪ 26740 41127 ▪ Closed Oct–May ▪ €€

An elegant restaurant specializing in fresh fish, Elli's can be found on the harbourside at Fiskárdo in a lovely old Venetian merchant's house. There's a good vegetarian menu, too.

5 Sirens Restaurant
MAP J4 ▪ Ithaki Yacht Club, Vathý, Ithaki ▪ 26740 33001 ▪ €€€

This nautical-themed restaurant with a fine wine list serves Ithakan favourites such as lamb and rooster cooked in clay pots.

6 Poseidon Fish Tavern
MAP J4 ▪ Vathý, Ithaki ▪ 69737 80189 ▪ Closed Nov–Apr ▪ €

One of Vathý's trendiest restaurants, Poseidon offers a range of specialities that include octopus, lobster and swordfish, along with homemade pies and meats cooked on charcoal.

7 Gourgouris Grill
MAP J6 ▪ Skála, Kefaloniá ▪ 26710 83584 ▪ €

Traditional stone-wall decor, tempting grilled dishes and a warm welcome ensure that Gourgouris Grill is always popular.

8 Vasso's, Fiskárdo
MAP H4 ▪ Fiskárdo, Kefaloniá ▪ 26740 41276 ▪ €€

The menu at Vasso's features inexpensive dishes, such as zucchini fritters and local meat pastries, as well as gourmet treats including linguine with langouste.

Dining at The Pines Restaurant

9 The Pines Restaurant
MAP J6 ▪ Skála, Kefaloniá ▪ 26710 83216 ▪ €

This bougainvillea-covered restaurant, with a terrace boasting lovely views, is a popular brunch and dinner venue. The food is a mix of international and local Greek cuisine.

10 Kyani Akti
MAP J4 ▪ Ioannis Metaxas, Argostóli, Kefaloniá ▪ 69776 45292 ▪ €

The aptly named Kyani Akti waterside restaurant (its name means "blue sea") serves the freshest seafood, and features Kefaloniá's signature dish – wine-stewed rooster.

See map on p84

TOP 10 Zákynthos

Religious icon from the Byzantine Museum

Zákynthos, the southernmost of the Ionian Islands, is famous for its unspoiled natural splendor – high cypress-covered mountains, dazzling beaches, magnificent sea caves – and a resident population of loggerhead sea turtles and Mediterranean monk seals. Owing to the 1953 earthquake that destroyed many towns and villages of the southern Ionian, few original buildings stand. However, the Venetian Fortress still overlooks the town, representing one of the stages of the long history of this splendid island.

ZÁKYNTHOS

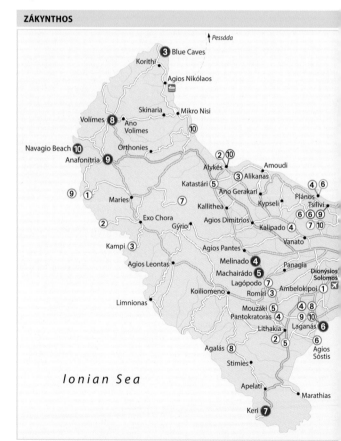

Ionian Sea

View of Zákynthos Town port

1 Zákynthos Town

One of many elegant squares in Zákynthos Town is its hub, Plateia Solomóu, from where most sights can be reached easily. Highlights include the Museum of Solomós, the Naval Museum of Zákynthos, and the fabulous Church of St Dionýsios, dedicated to the island's patron saint. A short walk north from the town centre, the Venetian fortress, perched above the town, offers impressive views (see pp32–3).

2 Byzantine Museum

Icons and frescoes saved from churches and monasteries damaged during the earthquake are on display at this superb museum, along with a scale model of a pre-earthquake Zákynthos. Key exhibits include *Descent from the Cross*, a painting from the Church of St Andreas of the Gardens; a 17th-century templon from the Church of St Demetrios of Kola; and a collection of sculptures dating from Hellenic and Byzantine times (see pp34–5).

3 Blue Caves
MAP K1 ■ Cape Skinári, Zákynthos

The Blue Caves, formed by the action of the sea on the coastline, lie at the northern tip of Zákynthos. The main cave, Blue Grotto, is overlooked by a pretty lighthouse, and is an amazing complex comprising two caverns that were discovered in the late 1900s. The caves look particularly breathtaking when the sun's rays shine in, turning the shimmering water a vivid shade of sapphire. They can be reached by boat from the village of Agios Nikólaos.

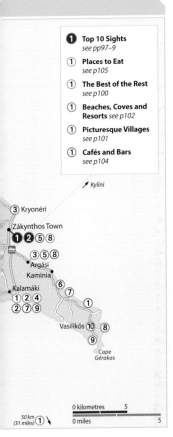

The stunning Blue Caves of Zákynthos

4 Melinado
MAP L2 ▪ Near Lagópodo, Zákynthos

A traditional village in the heart of the island, Melinado is surrounded by olive groves. Its elevated position, gives its outstanding views of the plains below. A mighty temple dedicated to the Greek goddess Artemis once stood here, and its remains can be seen today. Recent excavations have unearthed major finds, including architectural detailing and ancient coins. The ruins of a church lie here as well.

Church of Agia Mavra, Machairádo

5 Machairádo
MAP L2 ▪ Near Melinado, Zákynthos

The large village of Machairádo has been an agricultural community for centuries. Its centrepiece is a 14th-century church with a Venetian bell tower. Dedicated to St Mavra, a saint revered by the islanders, the Church of Agia Mavra has a notable collection of frescoes, a lavish iconostasis and many icons. One of the icons, called the Agia Mavra, is thought to be miraculous and worshippers kiss it as a mark of respect.

6 Gulf of Laganás
MAP M3 ▪ Off Laganás, Zákynthos

While often filled with watersports enthusiasts, the Gulf of Laganás is better known as the breeding ground of the endangered loggerhead turtle. After mating at sea, the females come ashore to lay their eggs at Laganás beach (see p100). The Sea Turtle Protection Association helps protect the breeding ground.

See map on pp96–7

ST DIONÝSIOS

The patron saint of Zákynthos island, St Dionýsios, was a monk at the Monastery of the Virgin Anafonítria (see p45) in the 16th century. He went on to become an Orthodox Christian Archbishop in Aegina, following a visit to the Holy Land. His remains are housed in a silver coffin in the Church of St Dionýsios in Zákynthos Town.

7 Keri
MAP L3 ▪ Limni Kerious beach, Zákynthos

The picturesque village of Keri, with its original stone houses built along meandering alleyways, lies high up in the hills to the south of the island. One of the few villages to escape the 1953 earthquake, Keri is popular with visitors who are keen to see the centuries-old lifestyle of the people of Zákynthos. Surrounded by vineyards and olive groves, it also produces some of the best wine and olive oil on the island, and offers great views of the sea.

8 Volímes
MAP K1 ▪ Northwest Zákynthos

An attractive village with much of its original architecture intact, Volímes lies in the mountainous northwest region of Zákynthos, a little inland from Navagio beach. It is divided in two – Ano (upper) and Kato (lower) Volímes. Its enchanting Venetian Baroque St Paraskevi church has a gilded iconostasis. Volímes' textile craftsmanship is also justly famous.

Monastery of the Virgin Anafonítria

9 Anafonítria
MAP K2 ▪ Near Volímes,
Zákynthos

With its vineyards and vine-covered houses, this pretty mountain village is best known for its connections to St Dionýsios, the island's patron saint, who was a monk at the Monastery of the Virgin Anafonítria (see p45). This well-preserved building has a medieval tower and a small church containing an ornate wooden iconostasis.

10 Navagio Beach
MAP K1 ▪ West coast, Zákynthos

Lying in a sheltered cove with soaring cliffs on either side, Navagio beach is world-famous, and a trip to Zákynthos would not be complete without taking the opportunity to visit this fine white-sand beach. Also known as Shipwreck Bay, which refers to the freighter that sits partially buried in its sand, the beach is reached by road from Volímes, or by boat.

Clifftop view of Navagio Beach

A DAY TRIP FROM ZÁKYNTHOS TOWN

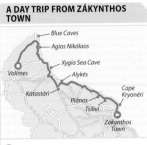

▶ **MORNING**

Start your day in the capital, **Zákynthos Town** (see p97), with a good breakfast at one of the many great tavernas on Plateia Solomóu. After breakfast, head north towards **Cape Kryonéri** (see p102) along the coast road, which offers breathtaking views of the Ionian Sea. Take in the resort of **Tsiliví** (see p100) en route, where you can stop for a cool drink and snack in one of its tavernas. Continue to the village-cum-resort of **Plános** (see p102), before arriving in **Alykés** (see p100). A superb beach that is popular with windsurfers, Alykés offers a wide selection of traditional tavernas. Stop here for a delicious lunch before continuing your journey.

AFTERNOON

Leaving Alykés and its lively holiday-makers behind, head inland to the island's largest village, **Katastári** (see p100). After leaving Katastári and driving north a short distance, you will arrive at a junction. You can either head west to **Volímes** or continue north on another, smaller mountainous road. You will see some amazing scenery and coastal views en route if you take the smaller road, passing the famous **Xygia Sea Cave** (see p100), with its sulphurous spring. Next, if you plan on seeing the famous **Blue Caves** (see p97) from the sea, look out for the signposts to the village of Agios Nikólaos, where you can catch a boat. After taking in the excellent views of the Blue Caves, head back via Volímes, or retrace your steps along the coast.

The Best of the Rest

① Strofades Islands
MAP M2 ■ SE of Zákynthos

These islands – Arpia, Stamfani and a few small islets – lie 60 km (37 miles) south of Zákynthos. They form part of the Zákynthos National Marine Park.

② Alykés
MAP L2 ■ Near Xygia beach, east coast, Zákynthos

The resort of Alykés is ideal for families with its numerous tavernas, long stretches of sandy beach, shallow water and varied watersports.

Taverna with sea views in Kampi

③ Kampi
MAP K2 ■ West coast, Zákynthos

To catch a true Zákynthos sunset, go to this traditional village. Spectacular sunsets can be seen at the top of the hill, where there is a big cross.

④ Kalipado
MAP L2 ■ NW of Zákynthos Town, Zákynthos

With its traditional stone houses, pretty churches and narrow streets, the village of Kalipado has changed little over the years.

⑤ Katastári
MAP L2 ■ Near Alykés, Zákynthos

The buildings on Katastári's main street follow the contours of the terrain down to the sea, giving the village the appearance of an amphitheatre. It offers stunning views of Alykés bay.

Sunset at Xygia beach, Zákynthos

⑥ Tsiliví
MAP L2 ■ Near Zákynthos Town, Zákynthos

Along with Alykés, the east-coast resort of Tsiliví is a magnet for holiday-makers. It boasts tavernas, restaurants, beaches, family attractions and a good selection of hotels.

⑦ Mount Vrachiónas
MAP K2

The 758-m- (2,500-ft-) tall Mount Vrachiónas is the highest point on Zákynthos. It lies at the centre of the island and is clothed in trees. Tiny villages, such as Gýrio and Loúha, are located around it.

⑧ Laganás Beach
MAP M3 ■ Gulf of Laganás, Zákynthos

This beach is the site where the female loggerhead turtles come ashore to lay eggs from May to August. The eggs are laid in deep holes and covered with sand.

⑨ Agios Ioannis Island
MAP K2 ■ W of Zákynthos

Lying just off the west coast at the entrance to Vromi cove, this off-the-beaten-track island is a haven for wildlife. From here you can enjoy great views of the coastline of Zákynthos.

⑩ Xygia Sea Cave
MAP L1 ■ Off Xygia beach, Zákynthos

The Xygia Sea Cave and beach is famed for its natural sulphurous springs. It is said that swimming in these waters is therapeutic.

Picturesque Villages

 Ambelokipoi
MAP L2 ▪ SW of Zákynthos Town

Largely a farming community, Ambelokipoi is delightful and has great mountain views. It is conveniently located near the island's airport and Zákynthos Town.

 Lithakia
MAP L3 ▪ Gulf of Laganás, Zákynthos

The charming hamlet of Lithakia is a resort in the making. The beach is quiet, the sea is shallow, and the handful of tavernas here are gradually growing in number.

 Romiri
MAP L2 ▪ N of Mouzáki, Zákynthos

A remote village that is blessed with panoramic views of the countryside to the east and the mountains to the west, Romiri is traditional and quiet.

 Pantokratoras
MAP L3 ▪ Near Lithakia, Zákynthos

Peaceful and scenic, this village, set in a verdant landscape of olive trees, provides visitors with the best of both worlds – a traditional way of life and a beach just a short distance away.

5 **Mouzáki**
MAP L3 ▪ N of Pantokratoras, Zákynthos

Established in the early 1500s, the unspoiled village of Mouzáki has a long history. Many traditions have been kept alive in this small community.

6 **Agios Sóstis Island**
MAP L3 ▪ Gulf of Laganás, S of Zákynthos

Linked to the shores of Laganás by a bridge, Agios Sóstis is a small island popular with families due to its lovely beach and calm, inviting waters.

The peaceful pretty village of Lagópodo

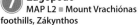 **Lagópodo**
MAP L2 ▪ Mount Vrachiónas foothills, Zákynthos

A small village surrounded by olive groves, Lagópodo is the place to head to if you want some peace and quiet. It is near the village of Machairádo.

8 **Agalás**
MAP L3 ▪ N of Keri, Zákynthos

The rugged coastline and forested valleys that characterize the south-west of Zákynthos form a scenic backdrop to this village. A traditional community, Agalás is known for preserving age-old customs.

9 **Kalamáki**
MAP M3 ▪ Gulf of Laganás, Zákynthos

Lying on the southern coast of Zákynthos, Kalamáki boasts one of the best beaches along this stretch of coastline. The village has fine sand and the sea here is shallow, making Kalamáki a favourite destination for families.

10 **Laganás**
MAP L3 ▪ Gulf of Laganás, Zákynthos

Best-known for its nightclubs, bars and lively visitors, this village is, in fact, a traditional community. Fishing was the only industry in Laganás before the advent of tourism.

See map on pp96–7

Beaches, Coves and Resorts

 Vromi Cove
MAP K2 ■ West coast, Zákynthos

A delightful indentation on the west coast, Vromi cove can be reached only by a small road from the village of Anafonítria. Agios Ioannis island (see p100) lies at its entrance.

 Exo Chora Cove
MAP K2 ■ Exo Chora, Zákynthos

The cove at the west-coast town of Exo Chora is quiet and unassuming. The town itself is a pleasure to visit, and has many original houses that survived the 1953 earthquake.

3 **Cape Kryonéri**
MAP M2 ■ Near Zákynthos Town, Zákynthos

Lying on the east coast about 1 km (half a mile) north of Zákynthos Town, Cape Kryonéri has a narrow pebble beach that runs down to the sea.

4 **Plános**
MAP L2 ■ Near Zákynthos Town, Zákynthos

Although a small village, Plános is fast developing into a popular holiday destination. It is one of the liveliest resorts on the east coast, with a soft sandy beach and calm water.

5 **Argási**
MAP M2 ■ S of Zákynthos Town, Zákynthos

Argási is a lively east-coast resort that has managed to retain its historic charm. It has a wide selection of excellent tavernas.

 Kaminia Beach
MAP M2 ■ Near Argási, Zákynthos

Located on the southernmost tip of the island, the quiet and undeveloped Kaminia beach offers good views of the tree-covered headland.

 Porto Zoro Beach
MAP M3 ■ Vasilikós peninsula, Zákynthos

If you love snorkelling, the striking rock formations at this quiet east-coast beach are worth exploring. It is considered to be one of the best beaches on the Vasilikós peninsula.

8 **Porto Roma**
MAP M3 ■ Vasilikós peninsula, Zákynthos

A tiny fishing harbour with a small pebbly beach and a handful of tavernas, Porto Roma lies on the southeast coast of the island. It is well known for its peaceful ambience.

9 **Gérakas Beach**
MAP M3 ■ Cape Gérakas, Zákynthos

Often referred to as the largest beach on the island, Gérakas, with its long sweep of golden sands, is also one of the best. The beach lies on the southernmost tip of Zákynthos.

10 **Vasilikós**
MAP M3 ■ Vasilikós peninsula, Zákynthos

The village of Vasilikós is renowned for its great beaches and excellent swimming conditions. It is the main community on the Vasilikós peninsula.

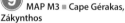

Beach on the Vasilikós peninsula

Outdoor Activities

 Diving and Snorkelling
The island's rugged coastline presents some fine opportunities for snorkellers to explore. Diving hot-spots include the Keri caves *(see p98)* and Kalamáki *(see p101)*.

Diving off the coast of Zákynthos

2 **Watersports**
Most major resorts offer all the usual watersports, including wind-surfing, water-skiing and jet-skiing. There may be restrictions around the breeding grounds of the endangered loggerhead turtle *(see p98)*, so visitors should be cautious in such areas.

3 **Sailing**
With minimal tidal variation and the gentle Mediterranean *maistro* wind blowing, the sea around Zákynthos is ideal for sailing enthu-siasts. There are numerous places to anchor on the island, and a marina at the port in Zákynthos Town.

4 **Archaeological Tours**
The island has many historic sites, such as Zákynthos Town's Venetian fortress *(see pp32–3)* and the ruins of a temple dedicated to Artemis at Melinado *(see p98)*. You can visit these on your own or with an organ-ized tour, available at most resorts.

5 **Cycling**
Most resorts have companies offering bicycles and mountain bikes for hire, but be aware that the rugged terrain can make cycling a difficult activity. Be sure to take plenty of water and a mobile phone with you.

6 **Turtle Conservation**
 www.archelon.gr
Visitors can join a marine turtle conservation project as part-time volunteers to monitor turtle nests and help spread awareness of the plight of the loggerhead turtles.

7 **Horse Riding**
Stables and small riding schools, such as Akrotiri Horse Riding Farm, can be found around the island. Several of these lie near Laganás *(see p101)* and Alykés *(see p100)*.

8 **Nature Trails**
Following a nature trail or creating your own can be a wonderful way to explore Zákynthos. Be sure to take a good, detailed map, walking shoes and plenty of water.

9 **Walking**
Some towns and villages on the island have designated walking routes. Alternatively, you can pick up a detailed map and devise your own route. A popular hike is from Plános to Alykés.

Swimmers arrive at a secluded beach

10 **Swimming**
This is popular on the island's beaches, and is generally very safe. However, be aware that some beaches may shelve steeply. Those on the east and south coast are generally safer.

See map on pp96–7

Cafés and Bars

Shaded setting at the Casa Playa Beach Bar

1 Casa Playa Beach Bar

MAP M3 ■ Banana Beach, Vasilikós Peninsula, Zákynthos ■ 0697 4758072

Looking out over the Ionian Sea's crystal water, this superb, trendy beach bar serves refreshing drinks all day long.

2 The Melon Bar

MAP M3 ■ Kalamáki, Zákynthos ■ 69381 98447

This popular spot in Kalamaki has a full food menu, chilled cocktails and a relaxed atmosphere.

3 Bliss Swimming Pool and Bar

MAP L2 ■ Alykana, Zákynthos ■ 69922 66266

Tasty home-cooked dishes elevate this wonderful swimming pool and bar. The drinks here are excellent quality and the service is great.

4 Seaside

MAP L3 ■ Laganás Beach, Zakynthos ■ 0697 4758072

A popular spot for sundowner cocktails, this lively bar beside the beach at Laganas also serves snacks and breakfast.

5 Base Café

MAP L4 ■ Plateia Agiou Markou, Zákynthos Town, Zákynthos ■ 26950 42409

More than just a café, Base is an institution in Zákynthos Town. It serves local drinks, cocktails and light snacks.

6 Paradise Cocktail Bar

MAP L2 ■ Tsiliví, Zákynthos ■ 26950 23190

Fun and fabulous cocktails are served at the friendly Paradise bar, which also has live music and entertainment.

7 Iguana Cocktail Bar

MAP M3 ■ Kalamáki, Zákynthos ■ 26950 22167

With a great view, live music, televisions and karaoke, this cocktail bar is the perfect place for a refreshing sundowner.

8 Thomas Elena Beach Bar

MAP M2 ■ Argasi, Zákynthos ■ 69743 48431

The menu at this welcoming beach bar has a wide range of snacks and drinks. Service is excellent and there are sunbeds and umbrellas on offer.

9 Planet Pub

MAP L2 ■ Tsiliví, Zákynthos ■ 26950 45106

You can dance to a variety of music, go for a swim in the well-lit pool or simply enjoy lively conversation over cocktails and light snacks at this landmark bar.

10 Olympic Bar

MAP L2 ■ Alykés, Zákynthos ■ 26950 83507

With contemporary, quirky decor, this stylish lounge bar offers local Greek drinks, such as ouzo, *tsipouro* and raki, cocktails and café-style cuisine, including breakfast.

Places to Eat

PRICE CATEGORIES

For a three-course meal for one with half a bottle of wine (or equivalent meal), taxes and extra charges.

€ under €30 €€ €30–€50 €€€ over €50

1 Zakanthi Restaurant

MAP M3 ■ Kalamáki, Zákynthos ■ 26950 43586 ■ €

Hearty grills and local dishes, such as souvlaki and salads, are on Zakanthi's menu. You can eat indoors or dine al fresco in the lush, subtly lit garden.

2 Essence Restaurant

MAP M3 ■ Kalamáki, Zákynthos ■ 69785 65232 ■ €€€

This upmarket restaurant serves Greek dishes with a twist, including meze sharing platters. Each dish can be paired with a complementing wine.

3 Flocas Café

MAP M2 ■ Argási, Zákynthos ■ 26950 24848 ■ €€

One of Argási's most stylish venues, the popular Flocas serves breakfast and other meals throughout the day.

4 Buon Amici

MAP M3 ■ Kalamáki, Zákynthos ■ 26950 22915 ■ €€

Buon Amici is known for its creative dishes, including pasta, seafood and meat in the finest Italian sauces.

5 Dennis Taverna

MAP L3 ■ Lithakia, Zákynthos ■ 26950 51387 ■ €€

Located in the centre of Lithakia and easy to find, this well-known family-run taverna has been running since 1976. It serves authentic Greek dishes.

6 M-eating

MAP L2 ■ Tsiliví, Zákynthos ■ 69820 43312 ■ Closed Oct–May ■ €€

Bright, modern and inviting are the best words to sum up M-eating. The upmarket menu is an eclectic mix of Mediterranean and Mexican cuisine, with some superb wines to match.

7 Zorbas Greek Taverna

MAP L2 ■ Tsilivi, Zákynthos ■ 69441 79512 ■ €€

With its stone walls and outside dining terrace, Zorbas is the quintessential Greek restaurant. Dancers and music combine with a lengthy menu of classic dishes. Chargrilled steaks cooked to perfection are a speciality.

8 Prosilio

MAP M4 ■ Panton and Latta 15, Zákynthos Town, Zákynthos ■ 26950 22040 ■ Closed Oct–May: Mon–Fri ■ €€

Enjoy fine food and wine while watching the lively drama of Prosilio's open kitchen. Menu classics include souvlaki and *pastitada*.

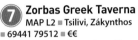

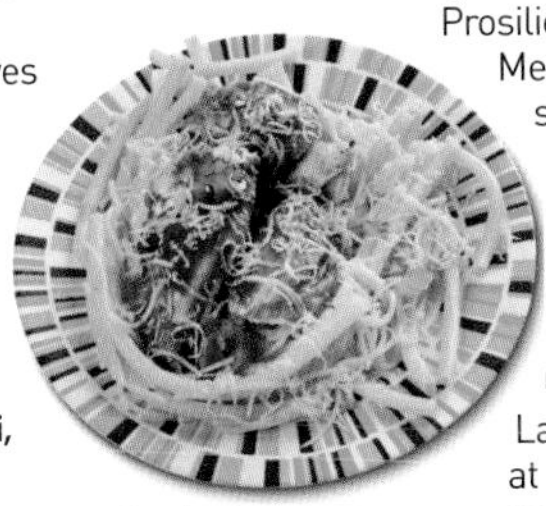

***Pastitada*, a tasty Greek chicken dish**

9 Panos

MAP L3 ■ Kalamáki Road, Laganás, Zákynthos ■ 26950 52685 ■ €€

Lamb *kleftiko* flambéed at the table is the signature dish at Panos, a trendy, acclaimed restaurant where diners eat on the pretty terrace. Fresh produce comes daily from the local market.

10 Premier Restaurant

MAP L2 ■ Tsiliví, Zákynthos ■ 26950 22411 ■ €€€

Well-prepared international and Greek dishes are beautifully presented at this popular Zákynthos restaurant.

See map on pp96–7

Streetsmart

A fashionable café on the Liston in
Corfu Old Town

Getting Around

Arriving by Air

From mid-April until late October or early November, the Ionian Islands are served by numerous charter flights from most British airports and many mainland European cities to **Ioánnis Kapodístrias Airport** on Corfu, **Dionýsios Solomós Airport** on Zákynthos and **Kefaloniá International Airport**. For Lefkáda, flights arrive at Preveza on the mainland, which is less than 30 minutes from the island by road via its causeway.

Outside the peak season, or from North America, Australia, Asia and Africa, you can fly to the islands via **Elefthérios Venizélos Airport (Athens)** with **Aegean Airlines** or **Olympic Air**. In summer, travellers from the USA and Canada could consider flying via London or other European airports.

Arriving by Sea

There are frequent international ferries to Corfu from the Italian ports of Venice, Ancona, Brindisi and Bari. These are large, modern vessels with a choice of accommodation in airline-style seats, second-class and first-class cabins. The crossing time is approximately 15–20 hours, and on the Ancona route there are views of the coasts of Croatia, Montenegro and Albania.

For most journeys, tickets must be bought in advance. There are numerous competing ferry lines, and schedules change monthly. Reservations can be made and tickets bought online through international booking sites such as **AFerry** and **Greek Travel Pages**. Both these offer frequently updated ferry schedules and general information about all Greek islands and ports serving Corfu and the Ionian Islands. Greek Travel Pages also has an online accommodation booking service.

Arriving by Road

Lefkáda's bridge and causeway make it possible to arrive by car or bus. Island-hopping around the Ionians with a car is not easy as many inter-island ferries do not carry vehicles, so it may become necessary to drive between mainland ports and take larger car ferries.

Domestic Sea Travel

The islands are linked with each other by an assortment of ferries. Numerous ferries connect Corfu with the major mainland ports of Igoumenitsa and Patras. For Kefaloniá, there are ferries from Patras and other mainland ports including Astakos and Kyllini. For Zákynthos, ferries sail from Kyllini. Inter-island ferries also connect Corfu with Paxí, Kefaloniá, Ithaki and Zákynthos. Reservations can be made through the Greek ferry operator **Blue Star Ferries**.

The Ionian Islands appear on many cruise ship itineraries. These huge floating hotels can often be seen anchored a little way off Corfu Town's coastline or at Zákynthos harbour. Smaller cruise ships depart regularly from Paxí and Antipaxí, Vasilikí on Lefkáda, Frikes Marina on Ithaki and Sámi Marina on Kefaloniá. There is also a wide choice of marinas and anchorages for private yachts.

Buses

Bus services in Corfu and the Ionian Islands are operated by **KTEL** (Κοινό Ταμείο Εισπράξεον Λεοφορείον), which publishes its timetables on its website. Visitors can save money on trips within Corfu Town and to nearby resort areas such as Dassia, Ipsos and Benitses by buying a book of five tickets at the main city centre bus terminus on Plateia San Rocco. Modern, air-conditioned **Green Buses Corfu** operate between Corfu Town and outlying resorts and villages. Larger towns have an internal bus network and intercity buses to Athens that include the ferry fare. Bus stations, where you can check timetables and buy tickets, can be found in the islands' main town harbours.

Most hotels and tour operators organize a range of excursions that take in the major sights. These trips usually include a running commentary giving historical and practical information. This can be a good way to see an island and learn about its sights. In some larger resorts, there are also mini tourist trains that ply the main sites.

Taxis

It is generally quite easy to find a taxi on any of the islands. The main towns have dedicated taxi ranks, and even the smallest villages have vehicles available to hire. Taxis are metered and inexpensive, and there should be a list of per-kilometre rates and allowable surcharges affixed to the dashboard. Make sure you negotiate beforehand if you want to hire one for a longer trip. Taxi drivers are obliged by law to issue a receipt for the total cost of a journey when the passenger requests it. It must clearly state the driver's name and the vehicle's registration number. Taking a taxi can be a good way to explore an island as the driver will almost certainly have plenty to tell you about local life.

Car Rental

A full driving licence held for at least a year is mandatory in order to rent a vehicle in Greece, however, for some classes of vehicles, it's necessary to have had a licence for at least three years. The minimum age for car rentals is 21 years, though some companies insist drivers must be over 25 years old. US licence holders must also carry an International Driving Permit. All the airports, resorts and some smaller towns have car rental offices, with global companies such as **Sixt**, **Europcar** and **Budget** well represented. You can hire a 4WD if exploring off-road, or a minibus if travelling with a group.

Driving is on the right, with priority from the right at junctions. Observe speed limits and take care when driving in mountainous areas or villages as the roadways can be quite narrow and uneven. Highways tend to be in good order. Children under 12 must not travel in the front seat.

Cycling

Most resorts have places where you can hire a bicycle or a mountain bike for a day, a couple of days or even longer. Reputable hire companies include **S-Bikes**, **Zákynthos Cycling Centre** and **Rent a Bike Kefaloniá**. Many tourist offices on the main islands will publish brochures with suggested cycle routes. Some are short, leisurely rides, while others are designed for more experienced cyclists and might cover long distances or challenging terrain. Always take plenty of water with you to avoid dehydration in the summer heat, and a fully charged mobile phone.

DIRECTORY

ARRIVING BY AIR

Aegean Airlines
w aegeanair.com

Dionýsios Solomós Airport
w zth-airport.gr

Elefthérios Venizélos Airport (Athens)
w aia.gr

Ioánnis Kapodístrias Airport
w cfu-airport.gr

Kefaloniá International Airport
w kefaloniaairport.info

Olympic Air
w olympicair.com

ARRIVING BY SEA

AFerry
w aferry.co.uk

Greek Travel Pages
w gtp.gr

DOMESTIC SEA TRAVEL

Blue Star Ferries
w bluestarferries.com

BUSES

Green Buses Corfu
w greenbuses.gr

KTEL
w astikoktelkerkyras.gr

CAR RENTAL

Budget
w budget.gr

Europcar
w europcar.com

Sixt
w sixt.com

CYCLING

Rent a Bike Kefaloniá
w rentabikekefalonia.gr

S-Bikes
w cyclecorfu.com

Zákynthos Cycling Centre
w podilatadiko.gr

Practical Information

Passports and Visas

For entry requirements, including visas, consult your nearest Greek embassy or check the **Greek Ministry of Foreign Affairs** website. EU nationals and citizens of the UK, US, Australia, Canada and New Zealand do not need visas for stays of up to three months.

Government Advice

Now more than ever, it is important to consult both your and the Greek government's advice before travelling. The **UK Foreign and Commonwealth Office**, the **US Department of State**, the **Australian Department of Foreign Affairs and Trade** and the **Greek General Secretariat for Civil Protection** offer the latest information on security, health and local regulations.

Customs Information

You can find information on the laws relating to goods and currency taken in or out of Greece on the **Greek General Directorate of Customs** and **Excise Duty** website.

Insurance

We recommend that you take out a comprehensive insurance policy covering theft, loss of belongings, medical care, cancellations and delays, and read the small print carefully. UK citizens are eligible for free emergency medical care in Greece provided they have a valid European Health Insurance Card (**EHIC**) or UK Global Health Insurance Card (**GHIC**). If you plan to rent a car, consider buying a stand-alone rental policy before leaving home, as this will be much cheaper than buying the rental company's cover.

Health

The healthcare system in Greece is made up of a mix of public and private health service providers, and standards can vary depending on your location. EU and UK citizens are entitled to free emergency medical care due to the reciprocal arrangements in place with Greece, but they will need to show a valid passport and valid EHIC or GHIC for registration at the hospital.

Medical facilities provided by the Greek national health service are generally good, but facilities on the smaller islands can be limited. In larger towns, hospitals are usually modern, with emergency and accident departments, and may have private medical practices.

In a medical emergency call an **ambulance**. Your hotel should be able to recommend local doctors who can assist with minor problems. For citizens of other countries, doctors' fees are payable immediately on treatment and a receipt will be given for insurance purposes.

Pharmacies in the Ionian Islands are indicated by a green cross. Consult a pharmacist for minor ailments. They are highly trained and, as well as giving advice, can prescribe and dispense some medicines. If you take prescription medicines, it is wise to pack enough for your stay as the local pharmacies may not stock the same medication. Call the out-of-hours **Pharmacies Hotline** for local pharmacy hours.

For information regarding COVID-19 vaccination requirements, consult government advice. No other vaccinations are required for travel in the Ionian Islands.

The sun can be very hot in the summer so wear sunscreen and a hat when outdoors, and drink plenty of water to avoid dehydration. It is generally safe to drink tap water, but it may be wise to buy bottled water to avoid an upset stomach through unfamiliar chemicals.

Mosquitoes do not carry serious diseases in Greece but they can leave a bite and transfer germs. It is a good idea to wear repellent, especially after dark.

Smoking, Alcohol and Drugs

In 2010, Greece introduced a law that officially banned smoking in enclosed public spaces, including in restaurants, bars and cafés. Smoking in out-door areas such as café terraces is usually permitted. Greek police will not tolerate rowdy or indecent behaviour, especially when fuelled by excessive alcohol consumption. Greek courts impose heavy fines or even prison sentences on people who behave indecently. Possession of narcotics is prohibited and could result in a prison sentence.

ID

Both locals and foreigners are required to have identification (either a passport or national ID card) on them at all times.

Personal Security

The Ionian Islands are a relatively safe destination to visit though petty crime can take place. Use your common sense and be alert to your surroundings, and you should enjoy a stress-free trip. Rental cars can be a target for criminals so make sure any valuables are locked in the boot. Keep passports, tickets and spare cash in hotel safes and lock hotel rooms upon exiting.

In the event of any incident – whether an accident, crime or otherwise – call the relevant emergency service.

Outbreaks of forest wildfires can occur in summer. Restricted access may be put in place in hazardous areas

As a rule, Greeks are very accepting of all people, regardless of their race, gender or sexuality. Homosexuality was legalized in 1951 and civil unions between same-sex couples have been legal since 2015. However, smaller towns and rural areas tend to be more conservative, and overt public displays of affection may receive a negative response.

Travellers with Specific Requirements

Greece has made some progress in meeting the needs of travellers with accessibility requirements, although facilities vary depending on the island. As of 2018, all hotels must by law provide at least one wheelchair-adapted en-suite room, though compliance, particularly in less touristy areas, tends to vary. Most museums have facilities for people with limited mobility, as do some beaches. A few places also have Braille or audio guides suitable for visually impaired visitors. Many island towns have ramps to access pedestrian crossings – when parked vehicles aren't blocking them – but announcements for the visually impaired to cross safely are rare.

Some specialist companies such as **Disabled Holidays** and **Enable Holidays** offer package holidays for travellers with specific requirements.

Time Zone

Greece is two hours ahead of GMT. It uses daylight saving time in summer – clocks go forward one hour on the last weekend of March, and back one hour on the last weekend of October.

Money

Greece's official currency is the euro (€). However, pound sterling is also readily accepted at some hotels and restaurants at a good rate.

Major credit cards are widely accepted by hotels, restaurants and shops, while prepaid currency cards are accepted in some. Contactless cards are now the rule – the Greek term for a card machine is *termatiko POS*. However, it is always worth carrying some cash as it is still preferred in some smaller establishments.

It is customary to tip up to ten per cent in restaurants if gratuity is not included in the bill; for taxi drivers, round up to the nearest euro. Consider tipping porters €1 per bag, housekeeping staff €2 for each day of your stay, and €1–2 for the concierges.

Electrical Appliances

The standard current is 230V/50Hz and plugs are usually of the two round pin variety (though some sockets take plugs with three round pins). If travelling from the UK you will need an adaptor. A transformer will also be required for some US devices. These are not always available locally, so pack what you need.

Mobile Phones and Wi-Fi

Mobile phone usage is widespread in Greece and visitors who bring their own phone are unlikely to experience any problems when calling home or a local number. If you have an international GSM-equipped phone, check with your service provider whether global roaming is available to you and what it will cost. You can also consider buying a local SIM card. EU visitors won't need to pay roaming charges. Main mobile providers include **Vodafone** and **Cosmote**.

The country code for Greece is 30. Most islands have their own codes: Corfu is 266, Kefaloniá 267 and Zákynthos 269.

Not all homes on the islands have an internet connection, although it is becoming more common by the day. Wi-Fi is widely available in most hotels, restaurants and bars for free or a small fee. Some towns and villages also offer free Wi-Fi hotspots (often in public buildings).

Postal Services

Post offices are run by **Elliniká Tahydromía (ELTA)** and can be found in all major towns and most villages. They are identified by the yellow signs that read *tachydromeia* (post office). Letter boxes are painted yellow. Opening times may vary between the islands, especially in villages, but are generally from around 7:30am until 2pm. Letters and postcards sent to European countries will usually arrive in around five days, but may take longer if posted from a remote village.

Weather

The Ionians have hot summers, mild autumns and springs, and cool winters. Temperatures rarely fall below 10° C (50° F) on the coast, but snow often falls in the mountains. December to February are the coolest, wettest months, while July and August are the hottest, with average temperatures of 26° C (79° F). Day temperatures can peak at over 40° C (104° F) at this time. **Meteo** is a great resource for weather forecasts.

Opening Hours

Opening hours tend to be vague in Greece, varying from day to day, season to season, and place to place. Shops are generally open from 9am until 9pm on weekdays, and close at 2pm on Mondays, Wednesdays and Saturdays. Small shops may also have a lunch break between 2pm and 5pm. Most shops outside of major resorts stay closed on Sundays. Banks are open from 8am until 2pm on weekdays and until 1:30pm on Fridays, but those in major tourist areas may stay open later. Restaurants usually open from 11am until 3pm for lunch, and from 7pm until 11pm for dinner, but are closed one day a week (the day varies). Opening times for museums and archaeological sites can vary quite a bit, but tend to be from 8am until 3pm Wednesday to Monday. Sites often extend their hours until 7pm in summer.

COVID-19 Increased rates of infection may result in temporary opening hours and/or closures. Always check ahead before visiting museums, attractions and hospitality venues.

Visitor Information

The **Greek National Tourism Organization (GNTO)** has offices in the UK, USA, Germany and many other countries. Address details can be found on the websites for each office or on the GNTO's own website. It has offices throughout the Ionian islands, including on Corfu, Paxí, Lefkáda, Kefaloniá, Ithaki and Zákynthos. For general information about the Greek Islands, **Greece Is** is a great resource. **The Hellenic Ministry of Culture**'s website and **Odysseus**, the official culture ministry site, provides information about archaeological sites, monuments, places of historical interest and museums.

Local Customs

The afternoon *mikró ýpno* ("little sleep") is sacrosanct, particularly in rural towns and villages: no public noise is allowed from 3pm to 5:30pm, and even making phone calls during these hours is frowned upon. Topless sunbathing is tolerated except in front of "family" tavernas, but nudity is restricted.

Language

Greek is the official language but English is widely spoken and taught from primary school, along with a second European language at secondary school. Locals do appreciate visitors' efforts to speak Greek, and a phrasebook may be helpful in more rural areas.

Taxes and Refunds

Usually included in the price, the top rate of FPA (Fóros Prostitheménis Axías) – the equivalent of VAT or sales tax – is 24 per cent in Greece, though taverna meals are assessed at 17 per cent. Visitors from outside the EU staying fewer than three months may claim this money back on purchases over €120. A Tax-Free form must be completed in the store, a copy of which is then given to the customs authorities on departure, along with proof of purchase.

Accommodation

It is advisable to book accommodation far in advance in high season, when prices can double in the major tourist centres. Smaller, off-the-radar places can be cheaper; some offer only bed and breakfast. Larger hotels also offer full-board and half-board options. Self-catering accommodation ranges from *diamerísmata* (studio apartments) and *enikiazómena domátia* (rented rooms) to large, purpose-built villas with fully equipped kitchens; the most expensive in Corfu even come complete with a chef. Many resorts in Corfu, Kefaloniá and Zákynthos offer all-inclusive packages with all meals, drinks, activities and accommodation included. Visitors during low season should note that most beachside accommodation is closed during this time, though there will be a few town hotels that continue to remain open.

DIRECTORY

MOBILE PHONES AND WI-FI

Cosmote
w cosmote.gr

Vodafone
w vodafone.gr

POSTAL SERVICES

Elliniká Tahydromía (ELTA)
w elta.gr

WEATHER

Meteo
w meteo.gr

VISITOR INFORMATION

Greece Is
w greece-is.com

Greek National Tourism Organization (GNTO)
w visitgreece.gr

Hellenic Ministry of Culture
w odysseus.culture.gr

Odysseus
w odysseus.culture.gr

Places to Stay

PRICE CATEGORIES
For a standard, double room per night (with breakfast if included), taxes and extra charges.

€ under €100 €€ €100–300 €€€ over €300

Luxury and Mid-Range Hotels in Corfu and Paxí

Bella Venezia
MAP P2 ▪ Corfu Town, Corfu ▪ 26610 46500 ▪ www.bellaveneziahotel.com ▪ €€
This elegant hotel is a glorious apricot-washed Neo-Classical mansion that was once the home of one of Corfu's foremost families. It has 31 exquisite rooms and a bar reminiscent of an English pub.

Kerkyra Golf Hotel
MAP E5 ▪ Alykés Potámou, Corfu ▪ 26610 24030 ▪ www.louishotels.com ▪ €€
Part of the Louis Hotels chain, this four-star family-orientated hotel lives up to its name with a complex that has swimming pools for adults and children, tennis courts, a playground and mini club for youngsters, plus an 18-hole golf course and a choice of restaurants. Accommodation includes 11 family rooms.

Marbella Corfu
MAP C3 ▪ Agios Ioannis, Corfu ▪ 26610 71183 ▪ www.marbella.gr ▪ €€
The five-star eco-friendly Marbella Corfu exudes understated luxury. The guestrooms are exquisite, and on-site facilities include a spa, a fitness centre, a swimming pool, a concert hall and several restaurants.

Paxós Beach Hotel
MAP B5 ▪ Gäios, Paxí ▪ 26620 32211 ▪ www.paxosbeachhotel.gr ▪ €€
Beautifully presented in local stone, this hotel overlooks one of Paxí's prettiest bays. Its terrace-restaurant offers panoramic views of the bay.

Corfu Palace
MAP P2 ▪ Leoforos Dimokratias 2, Corfu Town, Corfu ▪ 26610 23926 ▪ www.corfupalace.com ▪ €€€
Recognized around the world as one of Corfu's top hotels, this luxury palace stands in lush gardens overlooking Garitsa Bay. Its 115 beautifully appointed rooms and suites include facilities such as a marble bath.

Grecotel Corfu Imperial
MAP C3 ▪ Kommeno, Corfu ▪ 26610 88400 ▪ www.grecotel.com ▪ €€€
Sitting enticingly on a private peninsula overlooking the bay of Corfu, this charming five-star hotel offers fabulous sea-view rooms, an Italianate garden and private coves to explore. Facilities include gourmet restaurants and berthing for yachts.

Pelecas Country Club
MAP C4 ▪ Pélekas, Corfu ▪ 26610 52918 ▪ www.country-club.gr ▪ €€€
This luxurious retreat is set in a beautifully restored mansion with charming outbuildings, a summerhouse and stables. The main building dates from the 18th century.

Boutique Hotels in Corfu and Paxí

Casa Lucia
MAP C3 ▪ Sgombou, Corfu ▪ 26610 91419 ▪ www.casa-lucia-corfu.com ▪ €
An old olive press and its former outbuildings have been turned into these charming cottages set in pretty gardens in the quiet countryside.

Siora Vittoria
MAP P2 ▪ Corfu Town, Corfu ▪ 26610 36300 ▪ www.sioravittoria.com ▪ €
This Venetian-style townhouse was built in 1823 for the Metaxas family. It has just nine rooms, decorated simply but tastefully, and is equipped with luxuries including high thread-count linens, fluffy robes and designer toiletries.

Zefiros Hotel
MAP B3 ▪ Paleokastrítsa, Corfu ▪ 26630 41244 ▪ www.zefiroscorfuhotel.gr ▪ €
Redolent of Corfu in the 1930s, this classy hotel is is managed by a younger generation of the same family who opened it in 1935. It offers 11 rooms, all tastefully decorated and with gorgeous views.

Campsites in Corfu and Paxi

Dionysus Camping Village
MAP C3 ■ Darnilas Bay, Dasía, Corfu ■ 26610 91417 ■ www.dionysus camping.gr ■ €
Providing a choice of tents, bungalows and shaded places in which to shelter motor homes and caravans, this is one of the oldest and most popular campsites on Corfu. Amenities include shower blocks, a laundry, a supermarket and a restaurant.

Paleokastrítsa Camping
MAP B3 ■ Paleokastrítsa, Corfu ■ 26630 41101 ■ €
Set in the heart of the countryside, this campsite has shower blocks, electricity and a children's play area. Caravans, camper vans and visitors keen to sleep under canvas are welcome here.

Luxury and Mid-Range Hotels in Lefkáda

Grand Nefeli Hotel
MAP H2 ■ Ponti, Vasilikí, Lefkáda ■ 26450 31378 ■ www.grandnefeli.com ■ €€
Set in gardens that hug the beach, this apricot-washed hotel is a prominent complex on the coast at Vasilikí, a paradise for windsurfers. It has its own windsurfing tutors for those keen to try the sport.

Neion Hotel
MAP J2 ■ Kiafa, Alexandros, Lefkáda ■ 26450 41624 ■ www. neion.gr ■ €€
With its traditional Greek architectural features,

such as open fireplaces and wooden window shutters, this hotel comprises three stone buildings, which have all been beautifully restored. Located in the picturesque village of Kiafa, it boasts a dining terrace that looks out over a stunning rural landscape.

Porto Galini Hotel
MAP J2 ■ Maggana, Nikiana, Lefkáda ■ 26450 92433 ■ www.porto galini.gr ■ €€
This delightful hotel is made up of several small traditionally styled buildings, which are linked by walkways. It has sports facilities and a spa, along with well-presented guest rooms. The hotel welcomes children.

Portofico Hotel
MAP H2 ■ Ponti, Vasilikí, Lefkáda ■ 26450 31402 ■ www.portoficohotel.gr ■ €€
This family-run hotel is located beside the beautiful Ponti Beach and offers 29 charming guest rooms and a stylish restaurant dotted around a swimming pool and children's pool. All rooms have balconies and good facilities.

Captain Stavros
MAP J2 ■ Nydrí, Lefkáda ■ 26450 93333 ■ www. captainstavros-hotel.gr ■ €€€
Located in Lefkáda's lively town of Nydrí, the elegant Captain Stavros is the epitome of sophistication. The building resembles a ship, and the interiors are plush – they include a bar with a stained-glass ceiling. There is also an attractive swimming pool and terrace area.

Budget Stays in Lefkáda

Eva Beach Hotel
MAP J2 ■ Nydrí, Lefkáda ■ 26450 92545 ■ www. evabeach.gr ■ €
This small but pretty beachside hotel is ideal for family holidays. Among the amenities for children are highchairs, baby cots, a play area and a pool. The hotel is within walking distance of the resort's shops.

Ostria Hotel
MAP H1 ■ Agios Nikitas, Lefkáda ■ 26450 97300 ■ €
Sitting high above Agios Nikitas, one of the prettiest coastal villages on the island, this small pension-style hotel has 12 guest rooms, a restaurant and a bar decorated in traditional Greek style.

Vliho Bay
MAP J2 ■ Geni, Ormos Vlycho, Lefkáda ■ 26450 95619 ■ www.vlihobay. com ■ €
The decor in this hotel, which is set in a lovely bay just south of Nydrí, is traditional Greek. Most of its air-conditioned guest rooms are located around its swimming pool area.

Luxury and Mid-Range Hotels in Kefaloniá

Apostolata Island Resort & Spa
MAP J6 ■ Skála, Kefaloniá ■ 26710 83581 ■ www. apostolata.gr ■ €€
Set on a hillside gently sloping down to the sea, this hotel is one of the island's finest. Among its features are a spa and two good restaurants.

Ionian Plaza Hotel
MAP G5 ▪ Vallianou Square, Argostóli, Kefaloniá ▪ 26710 25581 ▪ www.ionianplaza.gr ▪ €€

This landmark hotel, set in a Neo-Classical building, stands in the centre of Argostóli. It overlooks a palm-tree-studded plaza, which becomes a hive of activity in the evening, when guests come to dine here, al fresco. The hotel has a plush and contemporary interior with well-appointed rooms.

Méditerranée Hotel
MAP G6 ▪ Lássi, Kefaloniá ▪ 26710 28760 ▪ www.mediter ranee hotel.gr ▪ €€

This hotel organizes sports, children's events and special Greek evenings for those who wish to hear traditional music and sample local fare. The view of the Lixoúri peninsula from the dining terrace is outstanding.

Porto Skála Hotel Village
MAP J6 ▪ Agios Georgios, Skála, Kefaloniá ▪ 26710 83501 ▪ www.portoskala.com ▪ €€

Designed to resemble a traditional Greek village, the brightly coloured studios here are positioned so all have a sea view. Swimming pools, a gym, Greek events and parties are just some of the draws.

Kefaloniá Grace Emelisse Hotel
MAP H4 ▪ Emplysi bay, Fiskárdo, Kefaloniá ▪ 26740 41200 ▪ www.emelissehotel.com ▪ €€€

Guests can enjoy luxury and seclusion at this chic top-end boutique hotel. Surrounded by cypress trees and located on the seashore, it has everything from gourmet restaurants and extensive sports facilities to an infinity pool.

Boutique Hotels in Kefaloniá and Ithaki

Alicelia Boutique Inn
MAP J4 ▪ Odyssea Androutsou, Vathý, Ithaki ▪ 26740 33695 ▪ www.alicelia-inn.gr ▪ €

With rooms decorated in pastel colours and furnished with comfortable beds, accommodation in this bijou hotel in Vathý includes family-sized suites for up to five people.

Korina Gallery Hotel
MAP J4 ▪ Telemachou 4, Vathý, Ithaki ▪ 26740 33393 ▪ www.korina ithacahotel.com ▪ €

A short walk from Vathý waterfront, this stylish small hotel in a traditional island mansion offers luxury facilities, including a pool. Accommodation is a mix of rooms and suites, some with whirlpool baths.

Perantzada Hotel
MAP J4 ▪ Odyssea Androutsou, Vathý, Ithaki ▪ 26740 33496 ▪ www.perantzadahotel.com ▪ €

This stunning hotel offers designer chic within a Neo-Classical building in Vathý's main port, surrounded by restaurants and bars. Rooms have balconies overlooking the sea. There is a pool, and water taxis to whisk you to nearby beaches.

Fiscardonna Luxury Suites
MAP H4 ▪ Fiskárdo, Kefaloniá ▪ 26740 41289 ▪ www.fiscardonna.com ▪ €€

Within an 1860s mansion on the Fiskárdo waterfront, this retreat is Kefaloniá's most stylish resort, adorned with satin, velvet, marble and gilt furnishings.

F Zeen Retreat
MAP H6 ▪ Lourdas, Kefaloniá ▪ 26710 31419 ▪ www.fzeenretreat.com ▪ €€

The fabulous F Zeen Retreat is adults-only. It has 28 beautifully decorated rooms set among tropical greenery, with two pools, a spa and an outdoor gym. Wellness activities include yoga, and there is a restaurant and bar, exclusively for the use of guests.

George Molfetas Museum Hotel
MAP H5 ▪ Faraklata, Kefaloniá ▪ 26710 84638 ▪ www.kefaloniamuseum hotel.com ▪ €€

The former home of a famed Kefalonián poet, this unique guesthouse with six rooms has been decorated and furnished with authentic antiques. Ingredients for the kitchen at this museum hotel are sourced from local organic farmers.

Roi Suites
MAP H4 ▪ Asos, Kefaloniá ▪ 26740 51001 ▪ www.apartmentsroi.com ▪ €€

Although slightly off the beaten track, this hotel offers a peaceful retreat with colourful sea-view rooms around a flower-filled courtyard. Harbourside bars and restaurants are within walking distance.

Thalassa Boutique Hotel

MAP G6 ■ Makrýs Gialos, Lassi, Kefaloniá ■ 26710 27081 ■ www.thalassa hotel.gr ■ €€€

Classy, minimalist rooms with gorgeous sea views are a highlight of this designer hotel close to one of Kefaloniá's most beautiful beaches and within easy reach of Argostolí. It also has a pool and a lush garden.

Luxury and Mid-Range Hotels in Zákynthos

Diana Palace

MAP M2 ■ Argasí, Zákynthos ■ 26950 23070 ■ www.diana hotels.gr ■ €€

This cosmopolitan hotel just outside Zákynthos Town, beside the beach at Argasí, promises a refreshing stay. With 140 well-presented guest rooms, it offers a wide range of facilities, including mini golf, a gym and a children's playground.

Hotel Palatino

MAP L4 ■ Kolokotroni St 10, Zákynthos Town, Zákynthos ■ 26950 27780 ■ www.palatino hotel.gr ■ €€

One of Zákynthos Town's best hotels, this four-star establishment has stylish rooms, its own café – the Palatino Café – and a cocktail bar. It lies just 100 m (300 ft) from the seafront.

Katerina Palace Hotel

MAP M2 ■ Argasí, Zákynthos ■ 26950 26998 ■ www.katerinapalace. com ■ €€

Conveniently positioned near the sea and close to Zákynthos Town, this hotel offers 105 well-equipped rooms designed with families in mind. All rooms afford views of the sea or the countryside. Greek-themed evenings are a speciality.

Phoenix Beach Hotel

MAP L2 ■ Tsiliví beach, Zákynthos ■ 26950 22483 ■ www.phoenix beachhotel.gr ■ €€

This elegant hotel stands right on Tsiliví's most popular stretch of beach. Rooms are individually designed and the reception and restaurant areas are lavishly presented.

Mabely Grand

MAP M2 ■ Kampi, Zákynthos ■ 26950 41302 ■ www.mabely. com ■ €€€

One of the finest hotels on Zákynthos, the Mabely Grand has an understated elegance. Guests can enjoy meals on the terrace overlooking the Ionian Sea, or try local dishes in the traditional Greek taverna.

Mediterranean Beach Resort

MAP L3 ■ Laganás, Zákynthos ■ 26950 55230 ■ www.med beach.gr ■ €€€

Located in the middle of the long sandy beach at Laganás, this large, modern hotel has everything for a lively holiday, with pools and leisure facilities, including a fully-equipped gym.

Boutique Hotels in Zákynthos

Boutique Aparthotel Galini

MAP K1 ■ Volímes, Zákynthos ■ 26953 01018 ■ www.boutiquehotel galini.gr ■ €

In the hills of nothern Zákynthos, this peaceful boutique hotel offers accommodation in half a dozen spacious traditional stone cottages, all with self-catering facilities. There is a small pool, with lovely views out to sea. However, visitors will need a car to commute back and forth from here.

Nobelos Boutique Hotel

MAP K1 ■ Agios Nikolaos, Zákynthos ■ 69441 48283 ■ www.nobelos.gr ■ €€

This hotel close to the island's northern tip has been converted from a traditional mansion. It offers just four luxury suites, a private beach and an organic restaurant.

Porto Zante Villas and Spa

MAP L2 ■ Tragaki, Zákynthos ■ 26950 65100 ■ www.portozante.com ■ €€€

Rated one of the best hotels in Greece, this hotel offers accommodation in gorgeous villas with private pools. The spa offers over 20 treatments. Dining options include the superb Asian fusion Maya Restaurant. For those who can afford it, this is the ultimate in luxury.

Index

Fiskárdo (Kefaloniá) (cont.)
places to stay 116
Flora
Korissíon Lagoon (Corfu)
20–21
Mýrtou Bay (Kefaloniá) 28
Foki Beach (Kefaloniá) 90
Folk Museum (Paxí) 43
Folklore festivals 58
Food and drink
budget tips 57
meze dishes 55
shops 92
where to eat 113
see also Restaurants;
Tavernas
Free attractions 56–7
French occupation 35, 38
Frikes (Ithaki) 88
Fryni Sto Mólos (Lefkáda)
54, 80

G
Gäios (Paxí) 6, 63, 65, 72, 73
places to stay 114
Galiskari Beach (Corfu) 47
Galloppi, Vincenzo 18
Gardiki Castle (Corfu) 6, 20,
66
George I, King of Greece 39
Gérakas Beach (Zákynthos)
102
Gerasímos, St 40, 45, 59
Gialos Beach (Lefkáda) 79, 80
Gidaki Beach (Ithaki) 90
Glass-bottomed boats 52
Golf 69
Good Friday 45
Gouvia (Corfu) 67, 71
Greece, union with 39, 58
Greeks, Ancient 38, 50
Grigorios Xenopoulos
Museum (Zákynthos
Town) 43
Guesthouses 113
Gulf of Laganás (Zákynthos)
98

H
Halikounas Beach (Corfu) 20
Health 110, 111
Hearn, Lafcadio 76
Hellenistic Agora (Mon
Repos) 17
Helmi's Natural History
Museum (Zákynthos
Town) 33
Herter, Ernst, Dying Achilles
19
Hiking see Walking and
hiking
Himare (Albania) 50

Historic sites 41
mainland 50–51
Historical and Folk Museum
(Argostóli) 87
History 38–9
Holy Saturday (Corfu) 59
Horse and carriage rides
(Corfu) 53
Horse riding 69, 91, 103
Hospitals 110
Hotels 113–17
Hydropolis (Corfu) 53

I
Icons 70, 92
Immigration 110
Insurance 110
International Folklore
Festival (Lefkáda) 59
International Music Festival
(Paxí) 59
Internet 111
Ioánnina 51
Islands, small 49
Issos Beach (Corfu) 21
Ithaki 7, 40
places to eat and drink 53,
54–5, 93, 94, 95
places to stay 116
see also Kefaloniá and
Ithaki
Itineraries 6–7
A Day Trip from Argostóli
to Fiskárdo 87
A Day trip from Corfu
Town to Paxí 65
A Day Trip from Zákynthos
Town 99
A Morning on the East
Coast (Lefkáda) 77
Seven Days in the Ionian
Islands 6–7
Two Days on Corfu 6

J
Jewellery 70, 92

K
Kalamáki (Zákynthos) 101,
104, 105
Kalámi (Corfu) 67
Kalamítsi (Lefkáda) 78
Kalipado (Zákynthos) 100
Kalvos, Andreas 43
Kampi (Zákynthos) 100, 117
Kantounes, Nikólaos 34
Karavomylos (Kefaloniá) 26
Kariá (Lefkáda) 78
Karminia Beach (Zákynthos)
102
Karyá (Kefaloniá) 89
Karya Museum (Lefkáda) 43

Kassiópi (Corfu) 6, 66, 72, 73
Kástro (Kefaloniá) 89
Katastári (Zákynthos) 99,
100
Katavothres Tunnel
(Kefaloniá) 26, 49
Katharon Monastery (Ithaki)
44, 57
Kathísma Beach (Lefkáda) 79
Kefaloniá 7
Argostóli **26–7**
beaches 46–7, 90
caves **30–31**
Mýrtou Bay Area **28–9**
myths and legends 40, 41
places to eat and drink 53,
54, 93, 94, 95
places to stay 115–17
see also Kefaloniá and
Ithaki
Kefaloniá and Ithaki 84–95
beaches 90
cafés and bars 94
A Day Trip from Argostóli
to Fiskárdo 87
map 84
outdoor activities 91
picturesque villages 89
places to stay 115–17
restaurants 95
shopping 92
sights 85–8
traditional tavernas 93
Keri (Zákynthos) 56, 98
Kioni (Ithaki) 60–61, 89
Kommeno (Corfu) 114
Kontogenada (Kefaloniá) 88
Korais, Ioánnis 34
Korgialeneio Historical and
Folklore Museum
(Argostóli) 27
Korgialeneios Library
(Argostóli) 26
Korissíon Lagoon (Corfu) 6,
10, **20–21**, 49, 65
Krini (Corfu) 67

L
Laganás (Zákynthos) 101,
105
beach 100, 104
places to stay 117
Lagópodo (Zákynthos) 101
Lake Avythos (Kefaloniá) 88
Lake Pamvotis 51
Lakithra (Kefaloniá) 89
Lákka (Paxí) 63, 65, 73
Language 126–7
Lássi (Kefaloniá) 27, 30
places to eat and drink 94,
95
places to stay 116, 117

Acknowledgments

Author

Carole French is an award-winning BBC-trained journalist, based in Cyprus and the UK. Her work has appeared in publications including *ABTA Magazine*, *Homes Overseas* and the *Daily Mail*. She has worked on numerous travel guides, and has provided expert consultation on the Greek Islands for television.

Additional Contributor

Robin Gauldie

Publishing Director Georgina Dee

Publisher Vivien Antwi

Design Director Phil Ormerod

Editorial Sophie Adam, Ankita Awasthi Tröger, Rachel Fox, Becky Miles, Rada Radojicic, Sally Schafer, Hollie Teague

Design Tessa Bindloss, Stuti Tiwari, Vinita Venugopal

Cover Design Richard Czapnik

Commissioned Photography Barry Hayden

Picture Research Taiyaba Khatoon, Ellen Root, Rituraj Singh

Cartography Jasneet Kaur Arora, Zafar-ul-Islam Khan, Suresh Kumar, Casper Morris

Senior Production Editor Jason Little

Production Igrain Roberts

Factchecker Robin Gauldie

Proofreader Laura Walker

Indexer Helen Peters

Revisions Ashif, Avanika, Shikha Kulkarni, Vagisha Pushp, Ankita Sharma, Anupama Shukla, Mark Silas, Priyanka Thakur, Penny Walker, Tanveer Abbas Zaidi

Picture Credits

The publisher would like to thank the following for their kind permission to reproduce their photographs:

Key: a-above; b-below/bottom; c-centre; f-far; l-left; r-right; t-top

123RF.com: Panagiotis Karapanagiotis 4cr; mkos83 48tl.

Alamy Stock Photo: ART Collection 33cr; 35ca; Gary B 53clb; Christopher Barnes 73crb; Steve Bentley 26bl, 87clb; Classic Image 38clb; Ian Dagnall 100cla, 104tl; Greg Balfour Evans 34cla, 42t, 52t, 96tl; PE Forsberg 12clb; Stephen French 81cra; funkyfood London - Paul Williams 2tl, 8–9; Olga Gajewska 99tl; Greece by Andy Newman 27cr; John Henshall 20–21; Heritage Image Partnership Ltd 41cl; Stephen Hughes 24–5c; Constantinos Iliopoulos 54tr, 76b, 80bl; imageBROKER 10cr; Will Ireland 4crb; Jeff Morgan 10 84tl; Jeff Morgan 13 30bl; Pawel Kazmierczak 3tl, 57cl, 60–61; David Kilpatrick 27tl, 32cla; Shirley Kilpatrick 93cra; Hercules Milas 6br, 11cra, 24cl, 43cl, 46bl, 77clb, 89cr; Martino Motti 66br; Remy Musser 16bl; Werner Otto 17tl; Nicholas Pitt 4clb; Prisma Archivo 10cl, 34br; Rolf Richardson 51clb; robertharding 74cla; Shopping / Peter Forsberg 56tl; David Tomlinson 67crb; Travel Pictures 69cra; Dimitris Vlassis 59tr; Jan Wlodarczyk 11cb; Gary Woods 11br.

Avalon: Michael Owston 72bl.

AWL Images: Robert Birkby 44tl, 64b; Matteo Colombo 11cr, 32–3; Neil Farrin 1, 18cr, 51b; Nick Ledger 63crb, 68t.

Depositphotos Inc: kwasny222 85cr; netfalls 78b; rachwal 103crb.

Dreamstime.com: Adisa 28–9, 86-7; Amlyd 18bl; Calin-andrei Stan 15tl; Mila Atkovska 2tr, 7tr, 36–7, 45cl, 97tl, 102b; Beijing Hetuchuangyi Images Co,. Ltd . 50br; Yuriy Brykaylo 29br; Ccat82 12cla, 20br, 49crb; Costas1962 16–17, 65cla; Paul Cowan 14–15; Simon Dannhauer; 20cla Davidzean 31tl; Tiberius Dinu 54cb; Dziewul 100br; Elenasfotos 12-3, 14cla; Fotomicar 26-7; Freesurf69 4b, 50t; Frizzantine 6cla; Stoyan Haytov 11ca, 88b; Fritz Hiersche 98cla, 101tr; Anna Hristova 28bl, 76tr; IrinaCharisma 33bl; Isselee 21bc; Panagiotis Karapanagiotis 4cla, 13clb, 19br; Karlosxii 10crb; Antonios Karvelas 25cra; Grzegorz Kordus 32clb, 41tr; Patryk Kosmider 48–9; Ksya 10bl, 19tl, 22–3; Lornet 63tl; Lucianbolca 4cl, 46t, 79tl, 79crb, 91t; Milosk50 10cra; Mkos83 30–31; Alexander Mychko 105cb; Nanookofthenorth 19c; Photostella 89tl, 90br; Slasta20 75b; Smoxx78 40tc; Tupungato 21tr; Tycoon751 55tr; Olena Vasylkova 59clb; Vasilis Ververidis 90cla; Vojtaheroutcom 47tr; Dennis Van De Water

56b; Wojphoto 4t; Anton Zelenov 44–5; Donka Zheleva 45tr; 58clb.

Garbis Jewellers: 92cl.

Getty Images: De Agostini / A. Garozzo 17cr; DEA Picture Library 38cr; Tim Graham 42bc; Hulton Deutsch 39bl; Imagno 39tr; Keystone 35bl; Holger Leue 57tr; David C Tomlinson 98–9; Tuul and Bruno Morandi 29tl.

iStockphoto.com: David Callan 58t; cunfek 85t; duncan1890 40b; Alina Iatiuc 75tl; kwasny221 97br; lucianbolca 25tl; milosducati 66cl; simonbradfield 82–3.

Maska Leather Workshop: 70cl.

Patounis Soap Factory: 43br.

SuperStock: age fotostock / Grant Rooney 3tr, 13tl, 106–107; imageBROKER / imageb / Helmut Corneli 103cla, / Norbert Probst 64cl, 69bl; robertharding / Tuul 47clb.

Taverna Agni: 71b.

Taverna Karbouris: 55bl.

Cover:
Front and spine: **AWL Images:** Neil Farrin
Back: **4Corners:** Reinhard Schmid crb; **Alamy Stock Photo:** Constantinos Iliopoulos tl; **AWL Images:** Neil Farrin b; **Dreamstime.com:** Tatiana Dyuvbanova cla, Aleh Varanishcha tr.

Pull Out Map Cover:
AWL Images: Neil Farrin

All other images © Dorling Kindersley
For further information see:
www.dkimages.com

Penguin Random House

First edition 2010

First published in Great Britain by Dorling Kindersley Limited, DK, One Embassy Gardens, 8 Viaduct Gardens, London SW11 7BW

The authorised representative in the EEA is Dorling Kindersley Verlag GmbH. Arnulfstr. 124, 80636 Munich, Germany

Published in the United States by DK Publishing, 1745 Broadway, 20th Floor, New York, NY 10019, USA

Copyright © 2010, 2022 Dorling Kindersley Limited
A Penguin Random House Company

23 24 25 10 9 8 7 6 5 4 3

Reprinted with revisions 2012, 2014, 2018, 2022

A CIP catalogue record is available from the British Library.

A catalogue record for this book is available from the Library of Congress.

ISSN 1479 344X

ISBN 978 0 2414 6269 0

Printed and bound in Malaysia

www.dk.com

As a guide to abbreviations in visitor information blocks: **Adm** *= admission charge;* **D** *= dinner.*

MIX
Paper | Supporting responsible forestry
FSC™ C018179

This book was made with Forest Stewardship Council™ certified paper – one small step in DK's commitment to a sustainable future.
For more information go to www.dk.com/our-green-pledge

Phrase Book

In an Emergency

Help!	Voítheia!	vo-ee-theea!
Stop!	Stamatíste!	sta-ma-tee-steh!
Call a doctor!	Fonáxte éna giatró!	fo-nak-steh e-na ya-tro!
Call an ambulance/ police/ fire brigade!	Kaléste to asthenofóro/ tin astynomía/ tin pyrosvestikí!	ka-le-steh to as-the-no-fo-ro/ teen a-sti-no-mía/ teen pee-ro-zve-stee-kee!
Where is the nearest telephone/ hospital?	Poú eínai to plisiéstero tiléfono/ nosokomeío?	poo-ee-ne to plee-see-e-ste-ro tee-le-pho-no/ no-so-ko-mee-o?

Communication Essentials

Yes	Nai	neh
Yes/No	Nai/Ochi	neh/o-chee
Please	Parakaló	pa-ra-ka-lo
Thank you	Efcharistó	ef-cha-ree-sto
Excuse me	Me synchoreíte	me seen-cho-ree-teh
Hello	Geiá sas	yeea sas
Goodbye	Antío	an-dee-o
Good morning	Kaliméra	ka-lee-me-ra
Good night	Kalinýchta	ka-lee-neech-ta
Morning	Proí	pro-ee
Afternoon	Apógevma	a-po-yev-ma
Evening	Vrádi	vrath-i
Yesterday	Chthés	chthes
Today	Símera	see-me-ra
Tomorrow	Avrio	av-ree-o
Here	Edó	ed-o
There	Ekeí	e-kee
What?	Tí?	tee?
Why?	Giatí?	ya-tee?
Where?	Poú?	poo?

Useful Phrases

How are you?	Tí kááneis?	tee ka-nees
Very well, thank you.	Poly kalá, efcharistó.	po-lee ka-la, ef-cha-ree-sto.
Pleased to meet you.	Chaíro polý.	che-ro po-lee.
Where is/are...?	Poú eínai...?	poo ee-ne...?
How far is it to...?	Póso apéchei…?	po-so a-pe -chee ...?
Do you speak English?	Miláte Angliká?	mee-la-te an-glee-ka?
I don't understand.	Den katalavaíno.	then ka-ta-la-ve-no.
Could you	Miláte lígo pio	mee-la-te lee-go
speak slowly?	argá parakaló?	pyo ar-ga pa-ra-ka-lo?
I'm sorry.	Me synchoreíte.	me seen-cho-ree-teh.

Useful Words

big	Megálo	me-ga-lo
small	Mikró	mi-kro
hot	Zestó	zes-to
cold	Krýo	kree-o
good	Kaló	ka-lo
bad	Kakó	ka-ko
enough	Arketá	ar-ke-ta
well	Kalá	ka-la

open	Anoichtá	a-neech-ta
closed	Kleistá	klee-sta
left	Aristerá	a-ree-ste-ra
right	Dexiá	dek-see-a
near	Kontá	kon-da
far	Makriá	ma-kree-a
up	Epáno	e-pa-no
down	Káto	ka-to
early	Norís	no-rees
late	Argá	ar-ga
toilet	Oi toualétes	ee-too-a-le-tes

Shopping

How much does this cost?	Póso kánei?	po-so ka-nee?
Do you have...?	Echete…?	e-che-teh...?
Do you take credit cards'/ travellers' cheques?	Décheste pistotikés kártes'/ travellers' cheques?	the-ches-teh pee-sto-tee-kes kar-tes/ travellers' cheques?
What time do you open/ close?	Póte anoígete/ kleínete?	po-teh a-nee-ye-teh/ klee-ne-teh?
Can you ship this overseas?	Mporeíte na to steilete sto exoterikó?	bo-ree-teh na to stee-le-teh sto e-xo-te-ree ko?

Sightseeing

tourist information	O EOT	o E-OT
archaeological	archaiologikós	ar-che-o-lo -yee-kos
art gallery	I gkalerí	ee ga-le-ree
beach	I paralía	ee pa-ra-lee-a
Byzantine	vyzantinós	vee-zan-dee-nos
castle	To kástro	to ka-stro
cathedral	I mitrópoli	ee mee-tro-po-lee
cave	To spílaio	to spee-le-o
church	I ekklisía	ee e-klee-see-a
folk art	laïkí téchni	la-ee-kee tech-nee
garden	O kípos	o kee-pos
gorge	To farángi	to fa-ran-gee
historical	istorikós	ee-sto-ree-kos
island	To nisí	to nee-see
library	I vivliothíki	ee veev-lee-o-thee-kee
monastery	moní	mo-ni
mountain	To vounó	to voo-no
museum	To mouseío	to moo-see-o
road	O drómos	o thro-mos
saint	ágios/ágioi/ agía/agies	a-yee-os/a-yee-ee/a-yee-a/ a-yee-es
square	I plateía	ee pla-tee-a
closed on public holidays	kleistó tis argíes	klee-sto tees aryee-es

Staying in a Hotel

Do you have a vacant room?	Echete domátia?	e-che-teh tho-ma-tee-a?
double room with double bed	Díklino me dipló kreváti	thee-klee-no meh thee-plo kre-va-tee
twin room	Díklino me moná krevátia	thee-klee-no meh mo-na kre-vat-ya
single room	Monóklino	mo-no-klee-no
key	To kleidí	to klee-dee
I have a reservation.	Echo kánei krátisi.	e-cho ka-nee kra-tee-see.

Eating Out

Have you got a table?	Échete trapézi?	e-che-te tra-pe-zee?
The bill, please.	Ton logariazmó parakaló.	ton lo-gar-yas-mo pa-ra-ka-lo.
I am a vegetarian.	Eímai chortofágos.	ee-meh chor-to-fa-gos.
What is fresh today?	Tí frésko échete símera?	tee fres-ko e-che-teh see-me-ra?
waiter/waitress	Kýrie/Garson"/Kyría	Kee-ree-eh/Gar-son/Kee-ree-a
menu	O katálogos	o ka-ta-lo-gos
cover charge	To "couvert"	to koo-ver
wine list	O katálogos me ta oinopnevmatódi	o ka-ta-lo-gos meh ta ee-no-pnev-ma-to-thee
glass	To potíri	to po-tee-ree
bottle	To mpoukáli	to bou-ka-lee
knife	To machaíri	to ma-che-ree
fork	To piroúni	to pee-roo-nee
spoon	To koutáli	to koo-ta-lee
breakfast	To proïnó	to pro-ee-no
lunch	To mesimerianó	to me-see-mer-ya-no
dinner	To deípno	to theep-no
main course	To kyríos gévma	to kee-ree-os yev-ma
starter/first course	Ta orektiká	ta o-rek-tee-ka
dessert	To glykó	ylee-ko
bar	To "bar"	To bar
taverna	I tavérna	ee ta-ver-na
café	To kafeneío	to ka-fe-nee-o
grill house	I psistariá	ee psee-sta-rya
wine shop	To oinopoleío	to ee-no-po-lee-o
restaurant	To estiatório	to e-stee-a-to-ree-o
ouzeri	To ouzerí	to oo-ze-ree
meze shop	To mezedopoleío	To me-ze-do-po-lee-o
take away	To souvlatzídiko	To soo-vlat-zee-dee-ko
kebabs		
rare	Eláchista psiméno	e-lach-ees-ta psee-me-no
medium	Métria psiméno	met-ree-a psee-me-no
well done	Kalopsiméno	ka-lo-psee-me-no

Basic Food and Drink

coffee	O Kafés	o ka-fes
with milk	ma galá	me ga-la
black coffee	skétos	ske-tos
without sugar	choris záchari	cho-rees za-cha-ree
medium sweet	métrios	me-tree-os
very sweet	glyk'ys	glee-kees
tea	tsái	tsa-ee
hot chocolate	zestí sokoláta	ze-stee so-ko-la-ta
wine	krasí	kra-see
red	kókkino	ko-kee-no
white	lefkó	lef-ko
rosé	rozé	ro-ze
raki	To rakí	to ra-kee
ouzo	To oúzo	to oo-zo
retsina	I retsína	ee ret-see-na
water	To neró	to ne-ro
octopus	To chtapódi	to chta-po-dee
fish	To psári	to psa-ree
cheese	To tyrí	to tee-ree

halloumi	To chaloúmi	to cha-loo-mee
feta	I féta	ee fe-ta
bread	To psomí	to pso-mee
bean soup	I fasoláda	ee fa-so-la-da
hummus	To houmous	to choo-moos
meat kebabs	O gýros	o yee-ros
Turkish delight	To loukoúmi	to loo-koo-mee
baklava	O mpaklavás	o bak-la-vas
kleftiko	To kléftiko	to klef-tee-ko

Numbers

1	éna	e-na
2	dýo	thee-o
3	tría	tree-a
4	téssera	te-se-ra
5	pénte	pen-deh
6	éxi	ek-si
7	eptá	ep-ta
8	ochtó	och-to
9	ennéa	e-ne-a
10	déka	the-ka
11	énteka	en-de-ka
12	dódeka	tho-the-ka
13	dekatría	de-ka-tree-a
14	dekatéssera	the-ka-tes-se-ra
15	dekapénte	the-ka-pen-de
16	dekaéxi	the-ka-ek-si
17	dekaeptá	the-ka-ep-ta
18	dekaochtó	the-ka-och-to
19	dekaennéa	the-ka-e-ne-a
20	eíkosi	ee-ko-see
21	eikosiéna	ee-ko-see-e-na
30	triánta	tree-an-da
40	saránta	sa-ran-da
50	penínta	pe-neen-da
60	exínta	ek-seen-da
70	evdomínta	ev-tho-meen-da
80	ogdónta	og-thon-da
90	enenínta	e-ne-neen-da
100	ekató	e-ka-to
200	diakósia	thya-kos-ya
1,000	chília	cheel-ya

Time, Days and Dates

one minute	éna leptó	e-na lep-to
one hour	mía óra	mee-a o-ra
half an hour	misí óra	mee-see o-ra
a day	mía méra	mee-a me-ra
a week	mía evdomáda	mee-a ev-tho-ma-tha
a month	énas mínas	e-nas mee-nas
a year	énas chrónos	e-nas chro-nos
Monday	Deftéra	thef-te-ra
Tuesday	Tríti	tree-tee
Wednesday	Tetárti	te-tar-tee
Thursday	Pémpti	pemp-tee
Friday	Paraskeví	pa-ras-ke-vee
Saturday	Sávvato	sa-va-to
Sunday	Kyriakí	keer-ee-a-kee
January	Ianouários	ee-a-noo-a-ree-os
February	Fevrouários	fev-roo-a-ree-os
March	Mártios	mar-tee-os
April	Aprílios	a-pree-lee-os
May	Máios	ma-ee-os
June	Ioúnios	ee-oo-nee-os
July	Ioúlios	ee-oo-lee-os
August	Avgoustos	av-goo-stos
September	Septémvrios	sep-tem-vree-os
October	Októvrios	ok-to-vree-os
November	Noémvrios	no-em-vree-os
December	Dekémvrios	the-kem-vree-os

Selected Ionians Map Index